CRACKS IN THE GREAT WALL

THE UFO PHENOMENON AND TRADITIONAL METAPHYSICS

BY THE SAME AUTHOR

Legends of the End:
Prophesies of the End Times, Antichrist,
Apocalypse, & Messiah from Eight Religious Traditions

The System of Antichrist: Truth & Falsehood
in Postmodernism & the Modern Age

Hammering Hot Iron:
A Spiritual Critique of Bly's Iron John

Doorkeepers of the Heart: Versions of Rabi'a

CHARLES UPTON

CRACKS IN THE GREAT WALL

❁

THE UFO PHENOMENON AND TRADITIONAL METAPHYSICS

SOPHIA PERENNIS

HILLSDALE NY

First published in the USA
By Sophia Perennis
Series editor: James R. Wetmore

Series editor: James R. Wetmore

For information, address:
Sophia Perennis, P.O. Box 611
Hillsdale NY 12529
sophiaperennis.com

Printed in the United States of America

Library of Congress Cataloging-in-Publication Data

Upton, Charles, 1948–
Cracks in the great wall: the UFO phenomenon and
traditional metaphysics / Charles Upton

p. cm.

ISBN 1 59731 024 7 (pbk : alk. paper)
ISBN 1 59731 020 4 (cloth : alk. paper)
1. Unidentified flying objects—Religious aspects. I. Title
BL65.U54 U68 2004
001.923—dc22 2004019282

CONTENTS

INTRODUCTION

At the present time the attempt to understand the UFO phenomenon seems to be going around in circles. The hypothesis that they are spaceships from other planets, the idea that they could be manifestations of 'fairies' or 'spirit-entities', and the suspicion that they may represent part of a government-sponsored mass mind-control program, chase each other in a maddening spiral, to no clear end. Much energy is expended in trying to make the Federal government 'come clean about what it knows,' but as UFOlogist Jacques Vallee has observed, the government is most likely covering up nothing but its own ignorance. Undoubtedly it has many more reports of the phenomenon in its archives than have been released to the public, but whether our wise rulers have been able to make any real sense of them is far from certain—though it is certainly in their interest to let us believe they have. The belief that their 'intelligence capabilities' stretch far beyond this planet, that the military-industrial priesthood is in touch with mysterious beings from beyond the stars, beings who possess fantastically advanced technologies, is certainly useful in order to subdue and terrorize the citizenry. 'Area 51' may or may not be a testing-ground for arcane, possibly 'psychotronic' technologies, but there is no question of its usefulness for social engineering. The government undoubtedly derives a great deal of valuable data from observing the myths and rituals evolved in relation to Nevada's 'Dreamland' by a frightened and mystified populace.

With hope for meaningful closure on the true nature of the phenomenon fading, those who have spent years pursuing such closure with little success have either sunk into a stunned, bitter cynicism about what has in some cases been their life's quest—a cynicism which fits right in with our contemporary 'postmodern' cynicism about the possibility of arriving at *any* kind of objective truth—or have opted instead for a worship of mystification itself, based on the feeling that if true mysteries still exist in this oppressive, modern, scientific world, things that not even science or the government can explain, then there is still 'hope'—a hope that would disappear if the phenomenon were even really understood. And so the quest to explain the UFO mystery becomes gradually and unwittingly transformed into the need to maintain it at any cost: 'The truth is out there—please don't let it get any nearer.' And so what started as a burning desire to explain the phenomenon is transformed to an active (though unconscious) resistance to the kind of comprehensive and adequate explanation which I believe this book provides. To fascinate oneself mysterious happenings may be entertaining, but it is also addictive, and ultimately ruinous to one's psychic health. If knowledge is possible, then it is always better to know.

The reason we find it so difficult to understand the UFO phenomenon is because we no longer understand the full structure of being. Earlier cultures understood, and every world religion still teaches, that material reality is only the lowest level of a universe composed of material, psychic, spiritual, and Divine domains. In the words of the late Fr Malachi Martin, from a letter to me in response to an earlier version of this book, 'precisely it is a question of metaphysical knowledge lacking that has queered the pitch for an understanding of what has been happening.' Science has a great deal to teach us about material reality, a certain modest amount to teach us about psychic reality, and nothing at all to teach us about Spiritual reality. Therefore no scientist, if he limits himself to science as it is presently defined, can give a comprehensive explanation of UFOs. Nor can psychic researchers and 'ghost busters' ultimately clear up the mystery. Both can make valuable contributions, but unless their findings are seen in the light of metaphysics, particularly traditional metaphysics, no closure can be reached. Nowadays the word 'metaphysics' conjures up images of ghosts, witches, spirit-entities, and—UFOs. Traditional metaphysics, however, is philosophy, often esoteric or mystical philosophy. Plato, Plotinus (Greeks) Shankara (Hindu), Nagarjuna (Buddhist), Ibn al-Arabi and Rumi (Muslims), Dionysius the Areopagite, Maximos the Confessor, Meister Eckhart and Dante Alighieri (Christians) were practitioners of traditional metaphysics.

When writing on traditional metaphysics, I draw largely on the writers of the Traditionalist or Perennialist School: René Guénon, A.K. Coomaraswamy, Frithjof Schuon, Titus Burckhardt, Martin Lings, Huston Smith, Rama Coomaraswamy, Wolfgang Smith, Joseph Epes Brown, Leo Schaya, Marco Pallis, Whitall Perry, James Cutsinger, S.H. Nasr, etc. And probably the writer most useful in helping us understand what UFOs are from the metaphysical perspective is René Guénon, who (along with Ananda Coomaraswamy) is usually considered to be the 'founder' of the Traditionalist School. Guénon, who died in 1950, investigated almost every occult or pseudo-esoteric group available to him in his native France before and after WWI: Spiritualists, Theosophists, Martinists, Neo-Gnostics, to name only a few. He emerged from his tour through the occult underworld of his time with an understanding that these groups were not simply childish and wrong-headed, but actively destructive to social stability and spiritual truth. At the same time, under the tutelage of fully-qualified teachers, he was studying the real teachings of the Hindu Vedanta, esoteric Taoism and Islamic Sufism as no one had ever done before in the Western world, at least in modern times, and rigorously separating them from the many fantastic and distorted ideas attributed to these eastern religions by various western occultists, notably those of the Theosophical Society. His ability to distinguish valid, comprehensive esoteric doctrines from the spurious concoctions of the occultists revealed to him the existence of what he called 'the agents of the counter-initiation'. He saw that behind many occult groups, largely populated by sincere but deluded spiritual dreamers, lurked much more sinister forces, forces consciously dedicated to the destruction of all true spiritualities, both exoteric and esoteric—even initiatory ones.

Guénon's writing stretched from profound expositions of 'pure' metaphysics and the doctrines of eastern religions to exposés of many aspects of western occultism and the various subversive and secret societies through which it operated—and continues to. And his prophetic masterpiece, in which he brought these two poles together, is *The Reign of Quantity and the Signs of the Times*, which becomes more relevant with each passing year. In this work he reveals the counter-initiation to be a precursor of the regime of the Antichrist, and its ultimate goal nothing less than the dissolution of the present world. A large part of what I have tried to do in the present book is to look at the UFO phenomenon—largely as presented by that most reliable and comprehensive of UFOlogists, Jacques Vallee —through the lens of traditional metaphysics, particularly that of Guénon's *Reign of Quantity*.

Another of Guénon's books is also valuable, however, for the historical light it throws on the belief in 'aliens' and UFOs. In *The Spiritist Fallacy*, Guénon shows how many twentieth-century spiritualists believed that discarnate spirits occupy space. He quotes one Ernest Bosc as calling them 'our friends in Space,' in response to an article in the spiritualist magazine *Fraternist* published in 1913. It may be significant that, fifty-five years later, the hippies were calling extra-terrestrials 'space brothers', and the New Age movement since the '70s has all but erased the distinction between space aliens and discarnate spirits.

Guénon mentions, as an example of the inflated pretensions of American spiritualists, a group calling itself the 'Ancient Order of Melchizedek'. He also speaks of an 'Esoteric Fraternity' in Boston led by the blind Hiram Butler.

Interestingly enough, this same Order of Melchizedek, as well as Hiram Butler—who also, as it turns out, established a group by the same name in California in 1889, on a communal farm in the foothills of the Sierras—make their appearance in *Messengers of Deception* (1979), by UFO researcher Jacques Vallee. Vallee investigated several groups, both in France and in the United States, calling themselves the Order of Melchizedek, and described the figure of Melchizedek, Abraham's master from the book of Genesis who had neither father or mother, as 'a symbol and a rallying point for saucer contactees'. So it seems possible that the widespread belief in UFOs, if not the proliferation of the phenomenon itself, are among the social and psychological fruits of the Spiritualist movement of the late nineteenth and early twentieth centuries, which is in so many ways the direct ancestor of the New Age movement of today.

In *The Spiritist Fallacy*, Guénon has this to say:

> [What] we see . . . in spiritism and other analogous movements, are influences that incontestably come from what some have called the 'sphere of the Antichrist'. This designation can also be taken symbolically, but that changes nothing in reality and does not render the influences less ill-omened. Assuredly, those who participate in such movements, and even those who believe they direct them, may know nothing of these things. This is where the greatest danger lies, for quite certainly many of them would flee in horror if they knew they were servants of the 'powers of darkness'. But their blindness is often irremediable and their good faith even helps draw in other victims. Does not this allow us to say that the supreme craft of the devil, however he may be conceived, is to make us deny his existence?[1]

As the reader will discover, I consider the contemporary UFO experience, and particularly the occurrence of 'alien abduction', to be the most direct manifestation conceivable of these powers of darkness—a manifestation which has become possible on such a widespread basis only because the present world-age is rapidly drawing toward a close: it is truly an 'end time' phenomenon. To demonstrate this, I have made use not only of the writings of René Guénon and Jacques Vallee, but also those of C.S. Lewis, Seraphim Rose, Frithjof Schuon, Whitall Perry, and Leo Schaya, with whose help I believe I have put together the most comprehensive and definitive explanation of the UFO phenomenon available today—though if anybody else can do better, then more power to him (or her); no one holds, or should hope to hold, the copyright on truth.

1. *The Spiritist Fallacy* (Hillsdale, NY: Sophia Perennis, 2004), p276.

UFOs and Traditional Metaphysics

When asked to define 'reality', William James gave the following answer: 'Anything is real of which we find ourselves obliged to take account of in any way.' According to this broad (though far from deep) definition, UFOs are certainly real. The mass belief in them has had an immense and incalculable effect upon our society. Nor has this belief simply materialized out of nothing; there is method behind this social, psychic, and empirically documented madness.

Friedrich Nietzsche said, 'Be careful: while you are looking into the abyss, the abyss is also looking into you.' This is why I caution the reader not to delve deeply into this book while in a state of depression, anxiety, or morbid curiosity. Whoever already knows how bad UFOs are, and is not required by his or her duties to investigate them, should ignore this information. Those who think there may be something 'spiritual' in them, however, and are not afraid of being seriously disillusioned, should read on.

The Place of the UFO Myth in Contemporary Culture

The UFO phenomenon constitutes a true postmodern demonology—though all too many of those who believe that Unidentified Flying Objects are extraterrestrial visitors treat it more as a postmodern religion. And the religious or quasi-religious relationship to the phenomenon is certainly not limited to the UFO cults *per se*. To take only one example: according to UFO researcher Jacques Vallee, in his *Messengers of Deception*,[1] the pope and founder of the Church

1. *Messengers of Deception* (Berkeley: And/Or Press, 1979).

of Scientology L. Ron Hubbard—who died in 1986 and who, according to my late '60s correspondence with ex-Scientologist William Burroughs, had a background in Naval Intelligence—'is said to have practiced ritual magic with a rocket expert named Jack Parsons, who met in the Mojave Desert in 1945 a "Spiritual Being" whom he regarded as a Venusian' (p13). According to Vallee, both Hubbard and Parsons had a background in the Ordo Templi Orientis, founded by black magician Aliester Crowley. Parsons, however, went on to become co-founder of both the Aerojet Corporation and the Jet Propulsion Laboratory.

Whether true or false, such assertions are right in line with the contemporary UFO folklore which informs us that our modern technology is either a 'gift' of the saucer people or a product of back-engineering from the saucer which supposedly crashed in Roswell, New Mexico in the 1947. And such beliefs to be found not only among New Age cults or eccentric hermits living in camping trailers; many 'responsible' and well-established computer professionals, and even corporate executives of our 'information culture', also hold them. For example, Joe Firmage, CEO of US Web/CKS, the two billion internet marketing and consulting firm he created, quit that position in 2000 to spread the UFO gospel. And at least one U.S. President, Jimmy Carter, admits to having witnessed a UFO. Ideas which were once the province of the 'lunatic fringe' are now increasingly acceptable among the political and corporate elite. So at the very least we can say that UFO mythology is on its way to becoming socially dominant, or at least highly significant, in today's global society—something mythographer Joseph Campbell was well aware of when he became 'mythic advisor' to George Lucas for his *Star Wars* trilogy.

The fact that I've had to delve deeply into traditional metaphysics in order to deal with the UFO phenomenon from a stable intellectual standpoint, and to criticize such beliefs as 'physical' time-travel and literal human reincarnation when dealing with the myth of 'aliens', shows the degree to which ideas which René Guénon called 'counter-initiatory' have occupied the centers of human consciousness abandoned over the past couple of centuries by traditional metaphysics and theology. According to Guénon, in his prophetic work *The Reign of Quantity and the Signs of the Times,* as this cycle of manifestation draws to a close, the cosmic environment first solidifies—this being in a way both the result and the cause of modern materialism—after which it simply fractures, because a material reality absolutely cut off from subtler planes of being is metaphysically impossible. These cracks in the 'great wall' separating the physical universe from the subtle or animic plane initially open in a 'downward' direction, toward the 'infra-psychic' or demonic realm (cf. Rev. 9:1–3); 'magical realism' replaces 'ordinary life'. It is only at the final moment that a great crack opens in the 'upward' direction, at the Second Coming of Christ, the advent of that Being whom the Hindus call the Kalki Avatara, who will bring this world to a close and inaugurate the next cycle of manifestation. And yet, for those with faith in God and an intuition of the Absolute, the 'upward crack', since it opens onto Eternity, is here already; though the mass mind is becoming less and less able to see it, the Door of Grace is not closed: 'Behold I am with you all days, even unto the consummation of the age.' As the dark shadow of a greater Light than this world can produce, the UFO phenomenon is truly an eschatological sign.

There is no question that the UFO myth has deeply affected the mass mind. When the Heaven's Gate cult committed group suicide near San Diego in the March of 1997, the question of the place of UFO ideology in contemporary life became, for a short time, the most compelling question confronting the American people. The followers of M.H. Applewhite, avid *Star Trek* fans, apparently believed that their souls would be reunited after death aboard a 'spaceship' which was invisibly following the Hale-Bopp comet. At the autopsy of the cult members, it was discovered that a number of the males had been castrated, an operation which was later claimed to have been voluntary.

There are some truths which it is shameful to know; the truth about UFOs is one of them. Even fifty years ago, such knowledge could only be encountered by someone pathologically attracted to human degeneracy and the dark side of the spiritual world. But today, what used to be the province of a few black magicians cannot be entirely avoided by any of us.

The UFO phenomenon is perhaps the most sinister complex of beliefs and events to be found among those loosely associated with the New Age. It has emerged from the shadows of pop science fiction and fringe occultism to become part of 'mainstream' American culture—as a belief-system or cultural 'archetype' if not a personal experience. The popular *X-Files* TV series, and the flood of 'New Age' books and publications which present teachings supposedly given by 'aliens'—*The Pleiadian Agenda* by Barbara Hand Clow, for example—are proof enough. In order to make sense of the phenomenon, I will waste no time in speculating whether or not it really is, or could be, occurring, but will simply accept the conclusions of reliable researchers in the field, notably Dr Jacques Vallee, and proceed from there. I will also accept, without apology, the existence of invisible worlds, and the ability of such worlds to impinge upon and alter the physical one. As Frithjof Schuon says,

> However restricted the experience of modern man may be in things belonging to the psychic or subtle order, there are still phenomena of that kind which are in no way inaccessible to him in principle, but he treats them from the start as 'superstitions' and hands them over to the occultists. Acceptance of the psychic dimension is in any case part of religion: one cannot deny magic without straying from faith.[1]

It is traditional Catholic doctrine, for example, to teach the reality of magic and witchcraft so that the faithful will be sure to avoid them. I would only add that where modern man denies the reality of psychic phenomena, postmodern man accepts them all too easily, and then uses them to rebel against religion, and finally to replace God.

To face the spiritual darkness which the UFO phenomenon represents and not be damaged, a kind of double consciousness is needed. To begin with, we will have to admit that such things as alien 'landings' and human 'abductions' are actually taking place. But we also need to remember that, as James Cutsinger says, 'there

1. *Light on the Ancient Worlds* (Bloomington, IN: World Wisdom Books, 1984), p104.

is a greater degree of Being in the beautiful than in the ugly.'[1] In the words of Schuon:

> Nothingness 'is' not, but it 'appears' with respect to the real, as the real projects itself toward the finite. To move away from the Divine Principle is to become 'other than He', while remaining of necessity in Him, since He is the sole reality. This means that the world necessarily comprises—in a relative fashion, of course, since nothingness does not exist—that privation of reality or of perfection which we call 'evil'. On the one hand, evil does not come from God, since being negative, it cannot have any positive cause; on the other, evil results from the unfolding of Divine manifestation, but in this respect, precisely, it is not 'evil,' it is simply the shadow of a process which is positive in itself.
>
> Finally, if we consider in *Maya* [i.e., Divine manifestation conceived of as having a partly illusory nature, of not being what it seems] the quality of 'obscurity' or 'ignorance' (*tamas*) as it is manifested in nature in general or man in particular, we are compelled to see in it what might be called the 'mystery of absurdity'; the absurd is that which, in itself and not as regards its metaphysical cause, is deprived of sufficient reason and manifests no more than its own blind accidentality. The genesis of the world in the first place, and the unfolding of human events, appear as a struggle against absurdity; the intelligible is confirmed as a contrast to the unintelligible.[2]

In other words, evil is like a hole in Being. In a sense it actually exists—you'd better not deny this, or you'll fall into the hole. But in another sense, it isn't real, since it is nothing but a lack or diminishment of reality, an empty space. The world of UFOs is like a waking nightmare, a world of dark unrealities made actual. But if we remember that beauty is more real than ugliness, and that Reality is good in essence, then we can—with God's help—look ugliness in the face and not be conquered by it, not finally *convinced*. Because,

1. *Advice to the Serious Seeker: Meditations on the Teachings of Frithjof Schuon* (Albany: SUNY, 1997), p34.
2. *Logic and Transcendence* (NY: Harper & Row, 1975), pp154–155.

as Schuon says, even though evil in its own nature is ultimately unreal, we still have to struggle against it. According to Schuon's pure metaphysics, evil is a product of that inevitable motion of being away from its Divine Principle which manifests as the cosmos. Just as light is always leaving the Sun *because* the Sun is radiant, shining ever more dimly into the surrounding darkness, so the very fact that God is not only Absolute but Infinite means that His Being must communicate itself, must eternally radiate in the direction of a non-being which can never be reached because it exists only as a tendency, not as a real part of Being. But the fact that, as Schuon says, we have to struggle against the constant pull of absurdity and non-being means that the doctrine of evil derived from his pure metaphysics must be balanced by the complementary doctrine that evil is always the product of an abuse of free will, by men or by spiritual beings. This apparent contradiction is resolved by the mysterious identity of choice and destiny, without which God's knowledge of our destiny would negate our freedom, rather than being His eternal and present knowledge of how we decide to use that freedom. And the fact that evil is 'unintelligible' does not mean that there is no order or method in it; if it were 'pure' chaos, it would not exist in even a relative sense. So evil cannot be absolutely unintelligible. It is better to describe it as *motion in the direction of* an absolute unintelligibility which, as pure non-being, can never be reached. Therefore, any organization or design which appears within evil is not part of its own nature, but has been stolen by evil from the Good. This is why true evil always exhibits a tell-tale mixture of diabolical cunning and immense stupidity.

In the first half of the twentieth century, the dominant image of extraterrestrials was that of horrible monsters from other worlds who arrive on Earth in spaceships to conquer and destroy. The representative book of this phase was H.G. Wells' *War of the Worlds*, published in 1898, which almost might be taken as prophetic of the First World War, when tanks, flame-throwers, poison gas and aerial bombardment first shocked the world with the horror of technological warfare. The power of this myth over the collective mind was amply demonstrated by Orson Welles' 'War of the Worlds' radio hoax in 1938, on the eve of World War II. (I've always been struck by the fact that both men had nearly the same last name; something was definitely 'welling up' from the psychic underworld.)

This image of extraterrestrials as inhuman monsters is still with us. But in the late 1950s it began to be supplemented by a radically different myth, that of the wise and powerful extraterrestrials who come to Earth to save us from nuclear self-destruction. The famous motion picture starring Michael Rennie, *The Day the Earth Stood Still* (1951) is the representative expression of this idea, which was the view of extraterrestrials dominant in the hippy movement. The hippy belief, appearing the second half of the '60s and inherited by the New Age movement some time in the '70s, had to do with the Space Brothers of the Intergalactic Council—in many ways the folk version of the United Federation of Planets from the *Star Trek* television series—who were either here to save the Earth, or to take all the good hippies away with them to a better world, in a counterculture version of the Evangelical Christian doctrine of 'the rapture'. And the 'Mothership' which was supposed to be hovering invisibly overhead, waiting to receive them, was (in my opinion) a distorted version of the Heavenly Jerusalem. The most detailed written expression of this belief-system was and is a massive 'channeled' text, *The Book of Urantia* (1955), and the myth of the benign extraterrestrial was also the basis of motion pictures like *Close Encounters of the Third Kind* (1977) and *ET* (1982).

Things began to change around the time when Whitley Strieber's sinister book *Communion* was published in 1986. With increasing numbers of reported 'alien abductions'—according to a 1991 survey, between several hundred thousand and several *million* Americans believe that they've been victims of such events—the concept of the benign Space Brother slowly began to be replaced by that of the demonic kidnapper, just as the cartoon cliché of the little green man with antennae on his head was turning into that of the 'gray', the corpse-colored, hairless being with huge, black, elongated eyes—an image derived directly from Strieber's descriptions, as depicted on the cover of his book. (UFO researcher Jacques Vallee describes this image as 'wise and benign'; to me it is bone-chilling.) I saw Strieber interviewed once on a PBS documentary. He admitted that his encounters with aliens were the most horrible events of his life, but showed absolutely *no desire to break with them* on account of this. The encounters were so strange and compelling that his fascination for them outweighed all other considerations—including, apparently, his own self-respect. I was reminded of the situation of the abused wife or incested child who can't imagine life apart from his or her abuser. It's a psychological truth that any extremely intense experience becomes 'numinous' in a sense. We tend to identify the most powerful things that have ever happened to us with 'reality' itself. The daughter raped by her father will carry this experience in her psyche as an indelible reference point, which in later life may lead her to demonize and/ or idealize other men in whom she sees, or upon whom she projects, aspects of her father. The soldier brutalized in war will seek out other violent situations—perhaps even making his living as a mercenary—because even though he knows that 'war is hell', he can't let it alone. 'Normal life' situations seem empty and unreal; nowhere but in the presence of bloody violence is he entirely 'himself'. He left part of his soul back on the battlefield and keeps returning to the place where he lost it. Only at the scene of the original crime does he feel, for a moment at least, complete.

THE PLACE OF UFOs IN THE HIERARCHY OF BEING

According to traditional metaphysics, as we have seen above, Being is arranged hierarchically, in discrete ontological levels. This is the 'Great Chain of Being' of the eighteenth century, which, when it 'collapsed'—when, that is, we started to see the hierarchy of Being horizontally in terms of time instead of vertically in terms of eternity—was transformed into the myth of progress. When we no longer recognized the Absolute as the eternal crown of the hierarchy of Being, we were forced to imagine that something bigger and better—or at least weirder and more powerful—lay in the Future. 'God *above*' was replaced by 'whatever is going to happen up *ahead*.' All spiritual traditions and traditional philosophies include the Great Chain of Being in one form or another, but since every metaphysician seems to render it a little differently, I'll take the risk of presenting my own version of it, which probably owes more to Sufi theosopher Ibn al-'Arabi and Traditionalist metaphysician Frithjof Schuon than anyone else, but can't strictly be attributed to either of them. It is based on eight levels of Being, in descending order. Each level not only transcends all that is below it, but also contains, in higher form, all that is below it. The first two levels are purely Divine, the second two Spiritual, the third two psychic, and the fourth two physical.

The Divine

The *first* level is Beyond Being (Dionysius the Areopagite), Godhead (Meister Eckhart), the unknowable Divine Essence.

The *second* level is pure Being, Allah ('the Deity'), God Himself—the personal God Who is Creator, Ruler, Judge and Savior of the universe, while transcending these functions absolutely, since He is not limited by any relationship with created being.

The Spirit

The *third* level is the Intellect, God's primal act of Self-understanding in terms of subject and object—in Christian terms, 'God the Father' and 'God the Son' (though, strictly speaking, Christian theology sees the Father and the Son as Divine Persons, and thus as aspects of the *second* level, above). Intellect is the ray of the Divine within the creatures—the *nous* of the Neo-Platonic philosophers—about which Eckhart said, 'there is Something in the soul which is uncreated and uncreatable.' In terms of its creative function, the Intellect is the *pneuma,* the Holy Spirit of God that 'moved on the face of the waters'.

The *fourth* level is the Archangelic, the realm of the permanent archetypes or Divine Names, perhaps represented by the Seven Lamps and the Four Living Creatures surrounding the Throne of the Lamb in the *Apocalypse.* This is the level of the eternal metaphysical principles or Platonic Ideas, which, far from being abstractions, are in reality more densely concrete—for all their transparency to the

Divine Light—and more highly charged with creative and truth-revealing energy than anything below them.

The Psyche

The *fifth* level is the Angelic, the manifestation of the Spirit on the psychic plane, the plane of thought, emotion and intent. Each angel is both a living, conscious individual and the manifestation of a specific Idea.

The *sixth* level is the Imaginal, the 'astral plane' or *'alam al-mithal*, where every thought, feeling or intent, whatever the level of being it essentially corresponds to, appears as a symbolic image which is at the same time a living being. This is the world of dreams and mental images, which is not simply happening inside this or that individual consciousness, but is continuous with an objective psychic 'environment', just as the human body is continuous with the natural world.

The Material World

The *seventh* level is the Etheric. This is the realm of the 'soul of matter', the hidden face of nature, the world of the Celtic *Fairies*, the Muslim *Jinn*, the world of 'bioplasma', of auras, of elemental spirits and subtle energies. It is the World Soul, the essential pattern and subtle substance of the material world.

The *eighth* level is the Material, the world reported by our senses.

Science deals almost exclusively with the eighth level, though it must sometimes confront phenomena emanating from the seventh, and theorize about seventh-level realities in order to explain apparent paradoxes appearing on the eighth. And since science has largely replaced religion and metaphysics as our dominant way of looking at the world, we are at a nearly total loss when it comes to explaining, and especially to *evaluating*, the UFO phenomenon. Because we believe in evolution and progress instead of understanding the eternal hierarchical nature of Being, *anything* that pops through from level seven to level eight, as far as we are concerned, might be

God, or Merlin the Magician, or a 'highly-evolved technological race', or God knows what. And the reason why so many seventh-level beings are now appearing to us, on a global level, may be *because* we have lost the ability to evaluate them; they can now represent themselves to us as anything they please.

WHO THE 'ALIENS' ARE

According to Muslim doctrine, The Jinn—plural of 'Jinni', the well-known spook from the lamp—are beings inhabiting a plane subtler than the Material but grosser than the Imaginal and Angelic: the *seventh* plane in the Great Chain of Being.

'Aliens' are members of the Jinn. According to Jacques Vallee, the most balanced and reliable of UFO researchers, who was invited to present his findings at a closed conference with U.N. General Secretary Kurt Waldheim (as recounted in his *Messengers of Deception*, which everyone interested in the UFO phenomenon should read), the phenomenon has three aspects. (1) It is a real, and inexplicable, phenomenon which appears on radar and leaves real physical traces. (2) It is a psychic phenomenon which profoundly affects people's perceptions. (3) It is surrounded by deceptions of the 'Mission Impossible' variety produced by actual human groups, apparently for the purpose of affecting mass belief. But how can we possibly put these three facts together? If UFOs are physically real, we say, then they must be spaceships. If they are psychic, then they must either be the product of mass hysteria, or real psychic entities. But if they are 'staged', then how can they be either? The mind grapples for closure. If they are spaceships, then we must turn to astronomy, NASA and the Defense Department for information on them. If they are subtle entities, then the psychics will tell us what they are up to. And if they are staged events, then we must rely on counter-intelligence and investigative reporting. But if they are all three...??? The critical mind tries to make sense of this, fails, and then shuts down. It is meant to.

Father Seraphim Rose, an American-born Eastern Orthodox priest who died in 1982, gives perhaps the best explanation of the

UFO phenomenon that we possess: Simply speaking, they are demons. They do what demons have always done. Their 'craft' are products of a demonic 'technology' which begins in the subtle realm and impinges on this one. He writes:

> The most puzzling aspect of UFO phenomena to most researchers—namely, the strange mingling of physical and psychic characteristics in them—is no puzzle at all to readers of Orthodox spiritual books, especially the Lives of the Saints. Demons also have 'physical bodies', although the 'matter' in them is of such subtlety that it cannot be perceived by men unless their spiritual 'doors of perception' are opened, whether with God's will (in the case of holy men) or against it (in the case of sorcerers and mediums).
>
> Orthodox literature has many examples of demonic manifestations which fit precisely the UFO pattern: apparitions of 'solid' beings and objects (whether demons themselves or their illusory creations) which suddenly 'materialize' and 'dematerialize', always with the aim of awing and confusing people and ultimately leading them to perdition. The Lives of the 4th-century St Anthony the Great (Eastern Orthodox Books, 1976) and the 3rd-century St Cyprian the Former Sorcerer (*The Orthodox Word*, 1976, no. 5) are filled with such incidents....
>
> It is clear that the manifestations of today's 'flying saucers' are quite within the 'technology' of demons; indeed, nothing else can explain them as well. The multifarious demonic deceptions of Orthodox literature have been adapted to the mythology of outer space, nothing more ... [their] purpose [is] to awe the beholders with a sense of the 'mysterious', and to produce 'proof' of the 'higher intelligences' ('angels', if the victim believes in them, or 'space visitors' for modern men), and thereby to gain trust for the *message* they wish to communicate.[1]

And lest the reader assume that only a traditional Christian monk

1. *Orthodoxy and the Religion of the Future* (Platina, CA: St Herman of Alaska Brotherhood, 1975), pp134, 136.

could gain this impression, Fr Seraphim quotes from the introduction to *UFOs and Related Subjects: An Annotated Bibliography*,[1] prepared by the Library of Congress for the United States Air Force Office of Scientific Research:

> Many of the UFO reports now being published in the popular press recount alleged incidents that are strikingly similar to demonic possession and psychic phenomena which have long been known to theologians and parapsychologists.[2]

Fr Seraphim, writing in the 1970s, relates the UFO phenomenon to the attraction of our culture as a whole to science fiction—a point which was driven home in 1997 when the Heaven's Gate cult, after committing mass suicide, were revealed as computer-savvy 'trekkies'. He writes:

> The future world and humanity are seen by science fiction ostensibly in terms of 'projections' from present-day scientific discoveries; in actuality, however, these 'projections' correspond quite remarkably to the everyday reality of occult and overtly demonic experience throughout the ages. Among the characteristics of the 'highly evolved' creatures of the future are: communication by mental telepathy, ability to fly, materialize and dematerialize, transform the appearances of things or create illusionary scenes and creatures by 'pure thought', travel at speeds far beyond any modern technology, to take possession of the bodies of earthmen; and the expounding of a 'spiritual' philosophy which is 'beyond all religions' and holds promise of a state where 'advanced intelligences' will no longer be dependent upon matter. All these are standard practices and claims of sorcerers and demons. A recent history of science fiction notes that 'a persistent aspect of the vision of science fiction is the desire to transcend normal experience ... through the presentation of characters and events that transgress the conditions of space and time as we know them' (Robert Scholes and Eric S. Rabkin,

1. By Lynn G. Catoe (Washington, DC: US Government Printing Office, 1969).
2. *Orthodoxy and the Religion of the Future*, p132.

> *Science Fiction: History, Science, Vision.* Oxford University Press, 1977, p175). The scripts of *Star Trek* and other science fiction stories, with their futuristic 'scientific' devices, read in parts like excerpts from the lives of the ancient Orthodox Saints, where the actions of sorcerers are described at a time when sorcery was still a strong part of pagan life.[1]

Fr Seraphim Rose repeats Jacques Vallee's hypothesis that UFOs 'are constructed *both as physical craft and as psychic devices.*' He also accepts Vallee's conclusion, based on a statistical analysis of only those sightings that are most convincing, that they can't be interplanetary spaceships because there are simply too many of them; it is not likely, for example, that the possibly two million Americans who have been abducted by aliens were kidnapped by astronauts. (Dr Vallee, as an astronomer, statistician, and computer scientist, is well equipped to carry on this kind of analysis.) But Fr Seraphim doesn't entirely explain Vallee's hard evidence for deception activities traceable to human groups, though his comparison of them to phenomena produced by the sorcerers of antiquity is highly suggestive. My own depressing hypothesis is this: Various groups of occultists or black magicians bent on world domination, some of whom seem to have ties with the intelligence community (see Vallee, *Messengers of Deception*, and *Revelations*)[2] and who may or may not possess 'inter-dimensional' technologies provided or inspired by the Jinn, are staging deceptions—the obvious propaganda by which the Roswell event has been sold to the public as the crash of an alien spaceship is a good example—for three purposes: (1) *to divert public attention from other activities they wish to hide; (2) to influence the mass mind toward a major paradigm-shift, away from religion and objective science, and toward belief in alien visitors*; and (3), *to invoke, by mass suggestion and sympathetic magic, the demons they worship.* The first two hypotheses were put forward by Jacques Vallee, who clearly documents, in *Messengers of Deception* and elsewhere, the

1. Ibid., pp103–104.
2. *Revelations: Alien Contact and Human Deception* (NY: Ballantine Books, 1991).

existence of just such groups and individuals clustered around the UFO phenomenon. The third hypothesis is my own. It may be that, early in this century, when literature on mass brainwashing first began to be published, books like *Man the Puppet: The Art of Controlling Minds* [Abram Lipsky, 1925] (which would likely have been available to Hitler and Mussolini, though this particular book seems to have been written by a Jew!), and when broadcast radio and early television were making instantaneous influence over the mass mind possible for the first time, certain black magicians realized that if they could invoke demons for themselves through self-suggestion, it might be possible to invoke them on a mass level through mass suggestion. They tried it, and it worked. They are still doing it. As an example of how such mass suggestion might work, psychiatrist John E. Mack, in his book *Abduction*, reports that one of his patients experienced an encounter with aliens soon after viewing a TV program based on Strieber's *Communion*; another recalled an abduction after reading the book itself. (I don't know enough to accuse Strieber of deliberate demonic invocation, or to exonerate him either; I only want to point out that highly-charged demonic images have a potent life of their own.) We should not conclude by this, however, that such wizards are powerful in the sense that they are more capable than the rest of us of autonomous action and choice. A psychotic arsonist or serial rapist may gain a *feeling* of great power, since it seems to him as if he is able to command the attention and vigorous action of the world around him. But it takes no power to roll a boulder down hill, or write a bad check; all it takes is an obsession that you can't control. True spiritual and social power is creative; it labors to build, to refine, to enlighten. But to ignite an entire forest with a single match is only the appearance of power; in reality it is nothing but deficiency of feeling, lack of intelligence, and weakness of will. To employ the metaphor of addiction, we can compare a true believer's or cynical manipulator's fascination with UFOs and psychic entities to the affects of alcohol or methamphetamine on the human system. Alcohol can produce a surge of emotional energy, amphetamines a similar explosion of physical and mental energy—but the reason we experience this energy is not because it is coming to us, but because it is leaving us. It's exactly the same in the case of those who invoke entities who are fundamentally less real—in the spiritual not the material sense—than human beings: the fascination we feel for them is not something they are giving us; it is something we are giving them, something they are stealing from us. If today's 'alien' shows many similarities to the traditional 'vampire', it is because both of them steal our 'blood', our life-energy, which in the most fundamental sense is nothing other than the spiritual attention we owe to God as the source of our life. As the adulterous affair destroys marriage by diverting erotic energy, so the 'alien' and the 'entity' destroy our relationship to God by diverting spiritual energy.

UFOs are 'apports'. Among the powers attributed to magicians and mediums has always been the ability to materialize objects. Such apports, however, tend to be unstable. They seem to exhibit all the characteristics of ordinary matter, yet they will often dematerialize again after a certain period. (Paramhamsa Yogananda's *Autobiography of a Yogi* is full of stories like this.) UFO phenomena exhibit the same property: undeniably real in a physical sense, they are also fleeting, as if the amount of energy required to maintain them on the material plane were too great to let them stay here for long; they are like fish out of water. And this is precisely in line with the folklore of the Jinn from all nations: they can affect the physical plane, but they can't exist here in any stable way. To hazard a wild speculation, I can let myself wonder whether our computer technology, which has always seemed to me partly inspired by the Jinn, may represent an attempt on their part to construct bodies for themselves that *are* stable in this world, particularly in view of the fact that the Jinn and the UFO aliens seem able to interact with electromagnetic energy: automobile engines die in close proximity to flying saucers; 'Raudive voices' appear spontaneously on magnetic tape, etc., etc. If so, it would also mean that—as in the de Maupassant story 'Le Horla'—they want to supplant us. But if they are so bent upon fascinating us poor, weak mortals with their superior powers, then why do they apparently envy our ability to occupy physical bodies? Could it be that they know full well that the Human Form is God's image and vicegerent on Earth—even if we ourselves have forgotten this—and are therefore doing all in their power to replace it, largely by tempting us to psychically and genetically deconstruct it? But if they, with all their 'wild talents', apparently want to be human, just as they seem to want to make us ever more Jinn-like, to turn us into 'changelings', what does this imply about their evaluation of their own state? Perhaps they simply want to get out of the Fire.

The 'aliens' do not require interaction with occultists and black magicians to appear in this world; but such alliances do make it easier for them, as well as providing them with conscious or unconscious agents willing and/or available to do their bidding. And the ability of these magicians to invoke alien entities on a mass level is simply one aspect of the quality of the time. According to René Guénon in *The Reign of Quantity and the Signs of the Times*,

> since all effective action necessarily presupposes agents, anti-traditional action is like all other kinds of action, so that it cannot be a sort of spontaneous or 'fortuitous' production.... The fact that it has conformed to the specific character of the cyclic period in which it has been working explains why it was possible and why it was successful, but is not enough to explain the manner of its realization, nor to indicate the various measures put into operation to arrive at its result.[1]

NOT ALL THE JINN ARE EVIL

Not all the Jinn are demons. According to Islamic doctrine, for example, some of the Jinn are 'Muslim' and some are not. The same distinction between benevolent and demonic entities can be found in Celtic fairy lore. The *Dakinis* of Tibetan Buddhism, for example—subtle entities in female form who help Tibetan yogis to attain Liberation—travel in a manner similar to UFOs, and are portrayed as entirely benign and helpful. In the story from the *Jetsün Kahbum* of the death of the famous Tibetan saint Milarepa,

1. *The Reign of Quantity and the Signs of the Times* (Hillsdale, NY: Sophia Perennis, 2004), p191.

> The *Dakinis* conveyed the *Chaitya* [the reliquary containing the saint's cremated remains] through the skies and held it directly above the chief disciples, so that it sent down its rays of light on the head of each of them.... And in the sky their appeared [the Tantric Deities] Gaypa-Dorje, Demchog, Sang-du, and Dorje-Pa-mo, surrounded by innumerable hosts, who, after circumambulating the Chief Deity, merged in him. Finally, the whole conclave resolved itself into an orb of light, and this sped away toward the East. The *Chaitya* ... was transported eastward, amid a peal of celestial music....[1]

Hindu *puranas* also mention travel in the subtle realm, on vehicles called *vimanas*; and such travel is not limited to demonic beings. Furthermore, the elemental spirits who form the connection between the natural world and its Creator are not evil, though they may be dangerous; the subtle, conscious archetype of a beautiful oak tree, for example, cannot be called a demon. (A friend of mine, incidentally, once saw—without benefit of psychedelics—a huge, brilliant green disc moving through the forest, passing through tree-trunks as if they were made of air: an elf-ship, apparently.) But the Jinn who are staging the present UFO manifestations almost certainly are demons. According to Seraphim Rose, they are here to prepare us for the religion of the Antichrist.[2] I agree—and I would add that anyone who wants to encounter psychic entities—good, evil or neutral—*because God isn't real enough to him* will become the demons' plaything. It may even be true, though I can't prove it, that those in the Neo-Pagan world who are attracted to the worship of elementals and nature spirits instead of the Divine Spirit may actually be seducing and corrupting those spirits, even if, to begin with, they are basically benign, or neutral. If you were being worshipped

1. *Tibet's Great Yogi, Milarepa: A Biography from the Tibetan*, ed. W.Y. Evans-Wentz (London: Oxford University Press, 1969), pp300–301.

2. A story was posted on the web a few years ago about UFO sightings over Chechnya; apparently a flight of saucers buzzed some of the Russian aircraft attacking the Chechen rebels. One of the rebels was quoted as saying: 'We don't know if they are angels or jinn, but they're on our side'—to which I would answer: 'They are definitely jinn, not angels – and their goal is to get *you* on *their* side.'

by thousands of devotees because they were fascinated by you and believed that their contact with you could give them magical powers, wouldn't you be seriously tempted? Wouldn't you be influenced to forget that your only duty is to remember God and obey His will?[1] The nature spirits are also duty-bound to remember and obey the Source of All Life; insofar as they do so, they become conduits which allow the Divine energy of the Holy Spirit to flow into and sustain the natural world. But if they forget that duty in their desire to fascinate and dominate their human worshippers, that flow of vital energy may be cut off. So it may be true that to worship the natural world, instead of contemplating God by means of it, is actually destructive to it, that an egotistical fascination for the nature spirits may in fact be the subtle-plane archetype of the destruction of the natural world by human greed and technology.

TIME-TRAVEL AND REINCARNATION RELATED AND DEBUNKED

The contemporary 'science fiction' myths of time-travel and multidimensional space, derived from imaginative speculation on Einsteinian and post-Einsteinian physics, and often applied to the UFO phenomenon, are in some ways replacing the world-view of the revealed religions, since they seem to transcend materialism and provide the 'miraculous' possibilities always associated with religious faith and spiritual experience. For God all things are possible—but if all things, or many strange things, are possible to UFOs, and will be possible to human science in the future, then who needs God? If space, time, matter, and even some mental processes can be manipulated by various subtle material energies, then who needs grace? If time-travel is possible, who needs eternity? This is

1. According to *surah* 72 of the Qur'an, known as 'The Jinn', verse 6: 'And indeed (O Muhammad), individuals of humankind used to invoke the protection of individuals of the Jinn, so that they increased them in revolt (against Allah).' From the translation by Mohammed Marmaduke Pickthall, *The Meaning of the Glorious Koran* (New York and Scarborough, Ontario: New American Library, 1953).

what is believed, and sometimes openly declared, by those who worship elemental energies via the cult of arcane science. But in reality the myth of time-travel, based for the most part on the belief that it might be possible to locally reverse the flow of time and travel 'backward', actually represents the death of the myth of progress. Here is evidence that if all coherent belief-systems are being deconstructed by post-modernism, not even scientism is immune to the process.

No less a speculative adventurer than Stephen Hawking has admitted his belief that time-travel is possible. But there are irreducible logical contradictions inherent in it, or at least in our usual way of conceiving of it. We imagine that it may be possible to travel in many directions in time instead of only one, just as we can travel in many directions in space. But if time travel will become possible in the future, then—by definition—it has already happened. And if it has already happened, then where are all the travelers from the future, all the historians, the archaeologists and the tourists? They are concealing themselves, we say, because their open appearance would be too shocking for us, and would alter future history. But if they are traveling from 'then' to 'now', they have already altered future history, whether they appear openly or not. And if future history has been altered by their time-travel, then it was 'always' altered. And if it was 'always' altered, then no 'alteration' has in fact taken place.

But others maintain that they *have* shown themselves, that the 'aliens' now appearing are really travelers to 'now' from our own future time. Why have they come back? Perhaps for the very purpose of altering history, of saving the human race from self-destruction. But if they fail in this attempt, then there will be no future human history for them to have traveled back from; and if they are destined to succeed, then they have already succeeded, so they never had to make the trip in the first place. They, and we, can relax.

Some try to solve the paradox of time-travel by claiming that it is possible to travel to an alternate or probable past, though not to the past we remember. But to 'travel' to a 'parallel' universe is not the same thing as to travel to one's own past. It may or may not be possible to separate, via arcane technology, the human body from it's own proper situation in time. But what then? That body would then enter the chaos of all probable space-times, with no way to 'home in' on any one of them, since its only way of 'tuning itself' to a particular space-time would be based on its entire structure, which is proper to only one region or quality of space-time. We and our lives are not two separate things—a truth that postmodern culture is doing all in its power to make us forget. Whether one is a yuppie who has thrown his or her home away to pursue the life of an itinerant globalist, or a refugee who is driven from his home by the forces of that same globalism, the post-modern human being is led to experience his or her ego as a self-enclosed monad with no organic relationship to its surroundings. And as we shift surroundings with ever-increasing frequency and emotional randomness, we begin to believe we can shift identities in the same way, that we can be whoever we 'play at' being, on a given day, or in a given moment. And so our identity either dissolves into a schizophrenic Robin Williams-like repertoire of 'postures' or 'routines', or else shrinks into a hard little kernel of impersonal, generic selfhood which we believe can be inserted indifferently into *any* situation because no situation is really native to it. Because our psyches are chaotic and fragmented, time-travel begins to seem possible to us, even natural, because we no longer experience our own *lives* as an integral part of our own *selves.*

If we are going to apply the metaphor of travel in space to travel in time, we will have to be thorough about it. And if we are, we will be forced to admit that if it is impossible to travel in space from San Francisco to New York if there is no New York there to go to, then it would be equally impossible for me to travel from now back to the Middle Ages unless there was a 'me' there in the Middle Ages for me to be.

But perhaps there was, we say. Perhaps I did lead a past life in the Middle Ages, and maybe I can travel back to it somehow. Here we can see how speculation on the possibility of time-travel makes it necessary, at one point, to posit the theory of reincarnation. If post-Einsteinian physics becomes our religion, then belief in reincarnation must, at one point, become a dogma of that religion. Now if I succeed in traveling back to the Middle Ages *physically*, then there must already exist, in potential, a record of the fact that I did so, that the 'me back then' appeared out of nowhere, or that a 'second me' appeared and encountered the 'me back then'. But if I were to discover this record, and later decide *not* to travel back in time, then where did the record come from? Where else but from a future time when I changed my mind and decided to go after all? This means that if I know there is a 'me' back there for me to go to, then I cannot decide not to go to him. And another way of saying 'I cannot decide not to go to him' is to say 'I *am* him'. And if I am him, then the concept of 'travel' becomes meaningless. On the other hand, obviously I am not him. I am myself. This self here and now cannot be super-imposed on that self there and then, because all selves, all forms, all moments, are unique, and are in fact the manifestation in the relative world of the Absolute Uniqueness of God. And so to ask if time-travel is physically possible is not like asking 'is it possible for me to travel from Spain to Germany?'; it is much more like asking 'is it possible for Spain itself to travel to Germany?' Who we are physically is inseparable from the time in which we live, because different times have different intrinsic qualities. According to Guénon in *The Reign of Quantity*,

> It is evident that periods of time are qualitatively differentiated by the events unfolded within them ... the situation of a body in space can vary through the occurrence of movement, whereas that of an event in time is rigidly determined and strictly 'unique', so that the essential nature of events seems to be much more rigidly tied to time than that of bodies is to space.[1]

If I exist in a different time, I must exist in a different state. My state as a newborn infant is inseparable from the year 1948; my state as a 48-year-old man is inseparable from the year 1997. The only way I can 'travel' to 1127 is for me to assume one of the states—that is, one of the individuals—available in 1127. So at the very least, time-travel cannot be physical.

But can it be psychic? Can it be reincarnational? Can a former incarnation of myself know me, by clairvoyant anticipation? Can I know him, by clairvoyant memory? Can we communicate with each other across the seas of multi-dimensional time?

1. *The Reign of Quantity*, p40.

Yes and no. That person in the Middle Ages is not me, nor am I him. As Guénon says in *The Spiritist Fallacy*, 'two identical things are inconceivable, because if they are really identical, they are not two things but one and the same thing; Leibniz is quite right on this point.' Still, we may have an eternal affinity for one another, because we are members of the same 'spiritual family', emanations from the same spiritual archetype or Name of God. This does not mean, however, that information—and, by implication, causality—can travel back through time from me to him. In reality, I simply inherit certain psychic 'material' from him, just as I would inherit the possessions of a deceased relative: psychic traits, unsolved problems, even memories. This is what is called 'metempsychosis', which is *not* the same thing as reincarnation. When inherited memories appear in my life, which can happen at any time from my birth until my death, it will necessarily seem to me as if I have, at least in a limited sense, gone back in time, since I am reliving another's past experiences. But in reality, those experiences have come forward in time to meet me, on the basis of an affinity—not an identity—between that past human being and myself, an affinity which in essence is eternal, not temporal. And he may also intuit my reality on the basis of the same eternal affinity, though in this case metempsychosis, or psychic inheritance, does not operate; if it did, memories of 'future' lifetimes would be just as common as memories of 'past' ones. He and I may discover our inner affinity over the course of our lives, by a seemingly temporal process—I by memory, he by anticipation—but the affinity itself is eternal in the mind of God; it exists beyond the plane of being where time, multidimensional or otherwise, has any meaning. So the only possible conclusion is that the myth of time travel, as well as the doctrine of reincarnation as a horizontal travel by the identical individual soul through time from one physical body to the next, is based on an inability to conceive of the real nature of eternity. Therefore, those who become obsessed with these myths are making themselves available to satanic forces whose goal is to hide from us the reality of eternity by means of a counterfeit, to so dazzle us with multidimensional spaces and multidirectional time-travel that we lose the ability to contemplatively imagine how God can see all things, past, present and future, as well as all probably realities, in an eternal present moment, as the 'Second Person of the Blessed Trinity', the total and integral form His Self-manifestation—in essence, not other than Himself—which, when refracted through the space-time matrix, we perceive by means of our physical senses, and name 'the universe'.

The Traditionalists, at least Ananda Coomaraswamy, René Guénon and Whitall Perry, deny the doctrine of reincarnation, and claim that, while it is accepted as true by many Hindus, and something resembling it by virtually all Buddhists, it is not orthodox teaching. They explain apparent references to chains of reincarnational existences as a misunderstanding, or misapplication, of the two distinct doctrines of *metempsychosis*—the teaching that psychic as well as physical material released by the dead (including memories) can be inherited by the living—and *transmigration*—the teaching that the eternal individuality passes through many states of existence by traveling vertically (or, to be strictly accurate, in an ascending or descending spiral) on the Great Chain of Being, never passing twice through any state, including our incarnate human one. According to Guénon in *The Spiritist Fallacy*,

> transmigration . . . is a question of the passage of the being to other states of existence, states that are defined . . . by entirely different conditions than those to which the human individual is subject. . . . That is what all the traditional doctrines of the East teach . . . the true doctrine of transmigration, understood according to the sense given it by pure metaphysics, that permits l the refutation of the idea of reincarnation in an absolute and decisive manner. . . .[1]

The Traditionalists maintain that not even Hinduism originally taught the doctrine of reincarnation as it is presently understood. Whitall Perry writes:

> the soul engaged in the *pitri-yana* ('Path of the ancestors') does not 'coast horizontally' through an indeterminate series of lives

1. *The Spiritist Fallacy*, pp178–179.

> and death[s], once having been 'launched' into the *samsara*, but rather is 'referred back' at the conclusion of each life to its Source; there is a vertical dimension (symbolized in the Upanishads as a return to the 'Sphere of the Moon'—equatable with *Hiranya-garbha*) which means a direct confrontation (but not yet identity) with its primeval point of Origin. Each 'life' can therefore be regarded as *original*, as a *fresh* entrance into existence or 'descent', whether into a splendid or a terrible domain, and as a unique cyclic experience with a return culminating in a *theophany* or 'Judgement', at which moment every soul does precisely—and with devastating clarity—recall its 'former life'. All the while the door of Liberation into the *deva-yana* ('Path of the gods') remains accessible to the 'Knowers of Truth', once the correct responses are given that allow passage out of the *samsara* and union with supra-formal states of being.[1]

In other words, I am not a 'reincarnation' of that man in the Middle Ages; in reality, both of us are unique 'incarnations', or facets, of the same eternal Archetype or 'Name of God'. Some uncertainty remains as to whether 'soul' in the above passage refers to the unique human individuality or the common Archetype of a whole 'family' of such individualities, but this is no more than a reflection of the primal ambiguity, or rather paradox, of the traditional Hindu doctrine of transmigration: that Brahman, the Absolute Itself, is 'the one and only Transmigrant'—a statement which is paradoxical because the Absolute, being beyond all relativity, is in another sense the only Reality which could not possibly transmigrate. This paradox is solved by the doctrine of *maya:* that *samsara*, though undeniably real from the point of view of the relative beings who experience it, is *illusion* from the point of view of the Absolute. God knows *samsara* as having no separate reality in itself; He sees it not as the joys and sorrows, the struggles and choices of numberless sentient beings—though He knows full well that those sentient beings actually experience it in this way, and knows this even more

1. 'Reincarnation: New Flesh on Old Bones' (*Studies in Comparative Religion*, vol. 13, nos. 3 and 4, p153).

deeply than they do themselves—but rather as the infinite self-manifesting radiation of Himself Alone. In other words, when I fully realize the truth that 'God is the one and only transmigrant,' transmigration ends. Furthermore, it is also known—because God knows it—that in Reality it never began.

The failure to realize that transmigration never began because 'the one and only Transmigrant' is the Absolute produces the ambiguous experience of transmigration, which, as a mode of *maya*, is 'both real and unreal'. The failure to understand that each transmigrational existence is a fresh creation—as in the Islamic concept of 'occasionalism', the doctrine that God re-creates the entire universe and the human soul in each new instant—produces the belief in reincarnation; vertical, and sovereign, Divine Act becomes horizontal, and contingent, cause-and-effect. The belief in reincarnation of the identical human individuality in a series of different lifetimes— a doctrine which, incidentally, is not taught by the Buddhists, since they do not posit a unique human individuality in the first place—severs the human soul from its transcendent Source, except at the first origin and the ultimate end of every indeterminate 'chain of lifetimes'. It results in a mechanistic and deistic universe where God can have no merciful, enlightening, forgiving and redeeming relationship with the worlds and the souls He has created—a universe where, because there can be no *dharma*, no saving Divine intervention, no religious dispensations, *karma* is absolute. I can neither repent, in such a universe, nor can God forgive. It was this absolutization of *karma* which led Mme Blavatsky (who, as we shall see, did accept reincarnation in her final work, *The Secret Doctrine*, despite denials by some of her followers) to hate and reject the Christian doctrine of the forgiveness of sins as a violation of the law of *karma*, and even to define prayer and sacrifice, conceived of as attempts to alter or circumvent *karma*, as acts of black magic. But to take *karma* as an absolute is absurd and self-contradictory. *Karma*, as the chain of causal actions and reactions in the relative world of *samsara*, is relative in essence; it can never be absolute. Every condition of causal inevitability on the horizontal plane can be compensated for by the operation of human freedom, and Divine Mercy, on the vertical one.

The doctrine of reincarnation is organically related to the belief in the possibility of time-travel. The mind of materialism, bound to space and time, confronts Eternity, but can neither realize nor understand it; materialism can only see 'another mode of existence' as 'another occasion of *material* existence.' The mind which is incapable of transcending time can conceive of such transcendence only as a greatly-enhanced ability to travel backwards, or laterally, across indefinite horizontal dimensions, to other material realities. The sense of what Sufis call the *waqt*, the eternal Divine Presence as manifest in this particular moment, threatens that mind's most fundamental assumptions, and thus its very existence. In flight from this Presence, it takes refuge in multidimensional spaces and parallel times and reincarnational chains-of-lifetimes. Such complex and arcane theories appeal to us because, simply, we are afraid to encounter God. We are reluctant to admit that this unique moment is eternally saved or eternally lost according to the present quality of our love, wisdom and vigilance, or, conversely, our hatred, delusion, and mental chaos. We want a second chance, or an infinite number of second chances, to be who we are in the sight of God. But if we are in flight from our integral identity *sub specie aeternitatis,* then all those second chances, all those future lifetimes or trips back to the past to clean up our act, are only so many new chances to go to Hell. Time is the Mercy of Eternity, said Blake. It is given to us as a precious gift, as part of our God-given human freedom. If we waste it, there is no second chance. The *desire* to travel in time in order to escape or alter the consequences of our actions is identical with the desire not to be here now, not to be who we really are, not to pay our karmic debts by no longer trying to escape our creditors, not to sit in the Spirit and allow our debts to be forgiven by God's Mercy, not to stand in the presence of God. It is, therefore, purely satanic. To sit in contemplation is to release the past to God and receive from Him the future; to 'travel in time' is to reject what God wants to give us and grab after what He wants to take away from us. In the words of the Sufi Shaykh Ibn Abbad of Ronda, 'The fool is one who strives to procure at each instant some result that Allah has not willed.'

Now it is true that, on the psychic plane, we already exist in a more multi-dimensional space-time than we do on the physical plane. If this were not true, visions of past and future realities, or of various 'parallel' realities, would not be possible, as clearly they are. But we can't 'travel' through these realities without transcending the perceptual framework necessary for physical reality, which includes linear, uni-directional time; and to transcend time is to transcend 'travel' itself, and enter simultaneity. To claim that we can transcend time in order to improve it, that we can travel to the past in order to create a better future, is like claiming that we can improve conditions inside our prison cell by being released from it. But who would assert that the best use of freedom, or even a possible use of it, is to ameliorate bondage? Who else but a deluded magician, who believes he can tap a higher level of being to reinforce the agendas of a lower one, that he can use Truth to manipulate his illusions, Desirelessness to fulfill his desires, Detachment to enhance his personal power? If we consciously realize that aspect of us which transcends the space-time limits of physical reality, then the whole field of physical space-time becomes virtually available to us. But it does not become available to that part of us which is still limited to space-time. The material level of our being which, while we live, is always there, and which always retains the potential to regain control of our total perceptual field, if we let it—the part which is always saying 'I'm afraid of getting old, I'm afraid of dying, I'm afraid of the end of the world, I've got to get out of here, I don't want to realize my limits, I don't want to face my end, why can't somebody freeze me so I can be revived in the future? Why can't somebody invent time-travel so I can get away into the past?'—that part of us cannot manipulate trans-material, multidimensional realities. It can never come into contact with them because, precisely, it is in flight from them. The only way for it to contact them would be for it to die to itself, and *that is the very thing it is attempting to establish contact with them in order to prevent.* This is the vicious circle of materialism attempting to access and control the Spirit for materialistic purposes, the contradiction inherent in the magical world-view, the self-defeating idolatry of subtle material forces and dimensions masquerading as the God-given freedom of the Spirit.

The Jinn do not transcend space and time, but rather exist in a different quality of space and time than we do in our day-to-day material lives. How this more multidimensional relation to the space-time matrix allows them to praise God in unique ways may never be known to us. But it is clear that those Jinn who are 'not Muslim' realize that if they can fascinate and/or terrify us with their own multidimensional reality, which we can never fully make our own in this life, it will powerfully distract us from our own proper relationship with space-time, and thus from the unique and specifically human responsibilities God has provided us with as ways to know Him: to be born; to grow 'in wisdom and age and grace'; in adulthood to struggle with the limitations of incarnate existence to protect and carry on life; in old age to acquire wisdom; at death, to meet our Maker. Whoever doesn't want to play by these rules no longer wants to be a human being; in the words of a 1975 speech, recorded by Jacques Vallee in *Messengers of Deception*, by a member of the Heaven's Gate Cult (or Human Individual Metamorphosis as it was then called), 'a lot of people are tired of playing the human game.' But the human game and the human form are the only way we can relate to the Divine Source of our lives; all the powers of the Jinn can't change this simple fact. But they can hide it from us, and that's exactly what they are presently trying to do. It is true that, on the psychic level of our being, we are every bit as multidimensional as the Jinn are. But it is also true that we are here in physical life for a purpose, that we are designed by God for physical experience as well as for psychic knowledge and Spiritual understanding, and that the purpose of physical life and uni-directional time is to continually present us with an eternal choice: to escape from the present moment, and so enter what the East Indian religions call 'Samsara' and the Abrahamic ones 'Hell', or to stand fully within it, and so ascend, by the vertical path which lifts us out of passing time, to 'Heaven', to higher states of reality. Whether the present activity of the Jinn to distract us from this ultimate human choice is better understood as subversion from their side or an abdication of the human mandate from ours need not concern us. But the eternal choice confronting us in this present moment *must* concern us. It is the 'one thing needful'. Religion has no other purpose but to remind us of it. Everything else is 'the outer darkness, where there will be weeping and gnashing of teeth.' It is nothing but a distraction—perhaps a fatal one. In *Messengers of Deception*, Jacques Vallee quotes a member of a UFO cult called The Order of Melchizedek as telling him, 'we must emphasize the fact that we are receiving a new program! *We do not have to go through the old programming of Armageddon.*' But Armageddon is precisely the ultimate battle between truth and falsehood, conceived of as confronting the entire human race at the same crucial moment. To avoid this battle—which the forces of evil would love to make us believe is somehow possible—is not to 'transcend truth and falsehood' (as if to equally mix reality and illusion were a sign of 'balance' and 'objectivity'), but simply to embrace falsehood, and so find ourselves, in the words of the Qur'an, 'among the losers'. And the attempt to circumvent God's judgement, to prevent the consequences of human action in this world from being fully confronted and penetrated by Divine Truth, is a central agenda of the New Age. To think we can avoid the battle of Armageddon is, however, to end up on the losing side.

UFO WORSHIP AS COUNTER-INITIATION

The interest in the figure of *Melchizedek* in the world of UFO cults, which is documented by Vallee in *Messengers of Deception*, is highly significant. Melchizedek had no father or mother, so he is, in a sense immortal: unborn, thus never to die. This would place him in the same category as the 'immortal prophets' Enoch, Elias and the Sufi Khidr, who is often identified with Elias. (As Melchizedek was Abraham's master in the Old Testament, so Khidr or Khezr is the name given by Sufis to the master encountered by Moses in the Qur'an.) According to Guénon in his book *The King of the World*, Melchizedek represents the Primordial Tradition, humanity's original and perennial knowledge of eternal Truth, the trunk of that tree whose branches are the major historical religions. *Enoch* is also big in the UFO world, since he—like Elias, and like the Prophet Muhammad, upon whom be peace—traveled to the next world without undergoing physical death. Such 'ascension' is a gift of God to a rare handful of his saints and prophets; UFO cultists, however, like to identify it with their own demonic 'abductions'. Contactee Jim Hurtak, for example, was given a text by his alien teachers which he published as *The Keys of Enoch*. UFO believers also regularly reinterpret Elias' 'fiery chariot' as a UFO.

In *The Reign of Quantity*, René Guénon spoke of the 'counter-initiation'— the attempt by demonic forces to subvert not only revealed religion, but also the more esoteric spiritualities, such as the Kabbalah within Judaism, Sufism within Islam, or Hesychasm within Orthodox Christianity—all of which, in their legitimate forms, are strictly traditional and orthodox, despite the heterodox distortions produced by people like Gurdjieff and Dion Fortune. In my opinion, the UFO phenomenon represents the most concentrated and wide-spread manifestation of this counter-initiation yet to appear, and the one most successful on a mass level. In Whitall Perry's *A Treasury of Traditional Wisdom*, we find the following clue to the interest of UFO cultists in Enoch, provided by 13th century German mystic Mechthild of Magdeburg:

It pleased Anti-Christ
To discover all the wisdom
Enoch had learned from God,
So that Anti-Christ could openly declare it
Along with his own false teaching:
For if only he could draw Enoch to himself
All the world and great honor would be his.[1]

According to the Traditionalist doctrine of The Transcendent Unity of Religions, all true revealed religions are renditions of the one Primordial Tradition which is as old as humankind. This Tradition, however, cannot be accessed directly, but must be approached via one of the major world religions—otherwise one will probably encounter one of the many attempts at a kind of 'generic' metaphysics, drawing upon fragments of many traditions, some system which represents itself as universal but remains cut off from the Wisdom and Grace of God, the only power which can make either a

1. Quoted in Whitall Perry, *A Treasury of Traditional Wisdom* (Cambridge: Quinta Essentia, 1991, p443).

sage or a saint. Although Truth is One, and the esoteric or mystical centers of all true religions point directly to this same Divine Truth, 'primordialism' cannot be a viable form in itself; the nourishing fruit grows on the branches of the tree, not the trunk. And, as the human door to Divine Reality, the Primordial Tradition can only be fully realized in the mystery of the soul's union with God. It would seem, therefore, that the prevalence of the figure of Melchizedek in UFO and Spiritualist lore is evidence of a satanic perversion of the Transcendent Unity of Religions. If the doctrine of the Unity of Truth can be falsely used to deny the providential efficaciousness of the particular Divine revelations which God has given, so as to promote a 'New Age' religious syncretism—as is in fact happening before our very eyes—then great damage will be done to the sacred forms which the Divine has established as paths for our return to the One who created us. And if the wide ways back to God are blocked (a blockage which, in God's mercy, can never be absolute), then the Powers of the Air, the nations of the *kafir* (unbelieving) Jinn, will have carte blanche to misrepresent the subtle, psychic plane as the Kingdom of Heaven, to replace wisdom with clairvoyance and sanctity with magical and psychic powers in the mind of the mass.

Melchizedek had no father or mother. As such, he symbolizes the primordial Unity of Being, ontologically previous to the pairs-of-opposites that determine manifest existence. The Satanic counterfeit of this transcendence-of-polarity, however, is the denial of polarity. Primordial Humanity, before the fall into time and space, was androgynous, as was Adam before Eve was separated. But the satanic counterfeit of the androgyne, was William Blake pointed out, is what he called the hermaphrodite. In Blake's system, Satan is an hermaphrodite in whom all possible states are chaotically mixed together—a perfect counterfeit of the Unity of Being, where all possibilities are embraced and synthesized by That which transcends them. What falls below polarity apes what transcends it. The figure of Melchizedek, as interpreted by the UFO-worshippers, is thus a satanic counterfeit of principial Unity, symbolizing, among other things, the destruction of sexuality, which modern genetics has now made possible. The self-castration of the members of the Heaven's

Gate UFO cult was an act of satanic worship: to destroy sexuality is to separate humanity from its archetype, and end its vicegerency.

RELIGION, EVOLUTION, AND UFOs

Jacques Vallee, in his book *Dimensions*[1]—possibly under the baneful influence of Whitley Strieber—speaks of the UFO phenomenon, inexplicable and numinous, as the likely origin of past, and maybe even future, religions. But in making this claim he exhibits what I can only call a shocking though very common lack of any sense of proportion, since he places in the same category demonic obsession, appearances of fairies, UFO encounters, and the apparition of the Virgin Mary at Fatima! This is like saying that whoever or whatever emerges from the same hotel—a saint, a swarm of flies, an automobile, a guide-dog, a drug-dealer or a can of garbage—must be of the same nature or have the same agenda. He is so mesmerized by the elementary fact, commonly accepted until quite recently by the vast majority of the human race, that measurable physical manifestations can emerge from the unseen, that the *quality* of what emerges entirely escapes him, largely because the *mechanism* of the emergence cannot be explained in present scientific terms—as if the divine miracles which are Christian or Muslim or Buddhist civilizations, lasting for centuries and millennia and representing the pinnacles of the human spirit, each one overflowing with exquisite art, profound philosophy, noble and dignified social mores, courageous heroism and self-sacrifice, and which continue to produce those mirrors of God in human form, our enlightened saints, could have been thrown together by a few spooks doing aerial acrobatics, abducting and brutalizing innocent bystanders, and raping a few women! I have the greatest respect for Dr Vallee as an objective, scientific and largely unprejudiced investigator of the UFO phenomenon, one who is at no pains to conceal his frequent horror and

1. *Dimensions: A Casebook of Alien Contact* (Chicago: Contemporary Books, 1988).

disgust at some of its manifestations; in *Confrontations*[1], for example, he has a chapter on the mysterious illnesses and deaths often associated with UFO contact. He seems to feel, however, that for the purposes of 'objectivity' he must be careful not to draw any conclusions from this disgust. But if one's normal disgust at rotten meat represents the 'organic wisdom' of the body, which is telling us that if we eat rotten meat we will get sick, then why can't he credit his emotional disgust at the UFO phenomenon as representing a similar wisdom of a psychic or Spiritual order? It is here that the limits of Vallee's scientific outlook, or rather his scientific ideology, his *scientism*, make themselves apparent. Because, according to the ideology of scientism—Guénon's 'Reign of Quantity'—it is not permitted to ask qualitative questions, or to base one's conclusions on qualitative considerations, *including morality*. To the degree that Dr Vallee is a good humanist, and therefore possesses a conscience and a sense of honor inherited from Christendom, though not credited to it, he is a man of culture. But one can only lament the complete lack of culture, and even of simple humanity, exhibited by those individuals—and that part of Dr Vallee—which can see and investigate nothing beyond the mechanism of things. Such a person must reduce an exalted religious doctrine and the incomparable civilization produced by it to a 'cultural overlay' on a basically material phenomenon. Moses saw a volcano and founded Judaism; the disciples of Jesus saw a UFO and built Christendom. But to someone with the slightest understanding of what a *religion* is, the vulgar and tasteless tricks produced by today's 'aliens', whose spiritual level seems in many cases to be little above that of the neighborhood child molester, when compared with those profoundly wise, good, and beautiful manifestations which are the world's religions and wisdom traditions—as awesome in aspect as they are sublime in conception—will necessarily appear as just so much excrement. And just because a piece of excrement is pulled like a rabbit out of a hat doesn't make it smell any sweeter. It is often said that 'there is no accounting for taste.' I disagree. A sound taste must be based on

1. *Confrontations: A Scientist's Search for Alien Contact* (New York: Ballantine Books, 1988).

some appreciation of the true, the good and the beautiful, which are ultimately nothing but the manifestation of God in this world, of which He alone is the Source. A degenerate taste, on the other hand, bespeaks a wounded soul—either traumatized, and so in need of healing, or deliberately depraved, and so headed for the wrath of God. I only pray that my own decision to write on the subject of UFOs does not indicate the beginnings of a similar depravity in me.

Nonetheless, Dr Vallee has done us a service in pointing out that many of the psycho-physical phenomena surrounding the appearance of the Virgin at Fatima are also commonly reported as part of UFO encounters: a perceived lowering of temperature, temporary paralysis, sweet fragrances, musical sounds, rainbow lights, the ambiguous aerial phenomenon known as 'angel hair' or 'the rain of flowers' (the last four being common features of apparitions of *devas* or *dakinis* in Vajrayana Buddhism), the descent of the object—in the case of Fatima, the sun—with a swinging motion, etc. Such similarities have led him to conclude that UFO manifestations and apparitions of the Virgin, or even the miracles and virgin birth of Jesus—since unexplained asexual pregnancies (which are in all likelihood demonic deceptions) are apparently sometimes reported in relation to 'alien' contacts, at least according to Vallee in *Dimensions*—represent the same order of phenomena. But anyone who expects a world-wide spiritual and cultural renewal such as that brought by Jesus of Nazareth to come from 'Rosemary's Baby' is deeply deluded. And the truth is, our actual expectations relating to such phenomena are often far from hopeful, whether or not we have the courage to admit it. Somewhere in our souls we all know the difference between the Son of God and the offspring of a demonic *incubus*; our horror movies, if nothing else, prove it. As for the psycho-physical phenomena surrounding apparitions both angelic and demonic, these are best understood as simple material or quasi-material reactions to the passage of a manifestation—*any* manifestation—from the psychic to the physical plane, past the energy-border called by some the 'etheric wall', which, when viewed from the material standpoint, seems in some way related to the electromagnetic spectrum, if we don't simply define it as the space-time matrix itself. It might be permissible in this context, at least provisionally, to re-define the classical 'four elements'—which are traditionally seen as the home of the subtle 'elemental spirits', the gnomes, undines, sylphs and salamanders—as *matter* (Earth, that which stabilizes physical manifestation); *energy* (Water, that which reveals waves in motion); *space* (Air, that which represents the subtle environment of all living beings); and *time* (Fire, that which germinates, transforms, and ultimately consumes, all things). Be that as it may, the truth is that we cannot fully evaluate a veridical apparition, in terms of either its original source or its ultimate consequences, simply by cataloguing the immediate psycho-physical reverberations of its breakthrough into our world. Such manifestations may be miracles, by which I mean that they have their source in the world of Spirit; they may be magical phenomena, having their source on the psychic plane alone; and, if magical, they may be either benign or demonic. In the words of Schuon, 'so far as miracles are concerned, their causes surpass the psychic plane, though their effects come by way of it'[1]—which means that all apparitions, though they may come from different points of origin, must enter our world through the same door; if this were not true, 'the discernment of spirits' would not be one of God's gifts, nor would Jesus have had to remind us that 'by their fruits you shall know them.'

Dr Vallee's scientism appears in the concluding chapter of *Dimensions*. The Introduction is written by Whitley Strieber; Vallee echoes him (unless Strieber is actually echoing Vallee) when, on p291, he states that: 'They [the UFO aliens] are . . . part of the control system for human evolution.' It is sad to realize that a dedicated researcher who values objectivity above all, and has consequently been able to question the dominant myth that UFOs are spaceships, and to credit not only their inexplicable physical reality, but also their undeniable psychic affects and the hard evidence for human deception surrounding them, without using one truth to hide the others, completely loses that admirable objectivity when it comes to the great idol of scientism, *evolution*. I will not recount the many discrepancies and contradictions in Darwin's doctrine, and in other variations of the belief, which an increasing number of scientists

1. *Light on the Ancient Worlds*, p104.

from many fields see as rendering the theory untenable, nor will I quote from the works of those Traditionalist metaphysicians, such as Frithjof Schuon, Martin Lings, Seyyed Hossein Nasr, and Huston Smith, who explain why such a conclusion is philosophically necessary. I will only ask Dr Vallee what the abductions, the weird medical experiments, the animal and human mutilations (which he reports in *Messengers of Deception*), the aerial acrobatics designed to awe and confuse, the sexual molestations, and the use of subtle forces, either psychic or psycho-technological, which paralyze the body and darken the mind, have to do with *evolution*? If we accept the theory of biological evolution, do we not understand it as based on physical processes which have no need of UFOs to help them along? And if we are talking about social or spiritual evolution, what do terror, violation and deception have to do with it? Can a monkey be forced to evolve into a man by torturing or hypnotizing him? Can a society be improved by confusing and terrorizing it? Can a man be forced to evolve into an angel by abducting and sexually molesting him? There is no 'material proof' that the UFO phenomenon represents a conflict between Divine and infra-psychic forces for the attention of the human mind and the allegiance of the human soul, a conflict which may well be the very one named 'Armageddon' in the book of the *Apocalypse*—nor will such proof ever be forthcoming. But I will submit that, to anyone surveying the phenomenon with the full range of his or her human faculties, the 'unseen warfare' hypothesis must appear an infinitely better explanation than the 'evolutionary' one.

MIND CONTROL AND *ROSWELL*: THE SPIELBERG AGENDA?

The deception and mind-control activities which cluster around the UFO phenomenon are discernible not only in staged manifestations of seemingly extraterrestrial landings or supernatural events, but also in certain media productions, particularly motion pictures like *Close Encounters of the Third Kind*. Anyone who is really interested in this hypothesis should go down to his or her video store and rent

Close Encounters, the *Star Wars* trilogy (1977; 1980; 1983), *ET*, *A Fire in the Sky* (1993) and *Roswell*. *A Fire in the Sky*, the story of a supposedly true-life alien abduction, is a fairly innocent and straightforward account of a intensely traumatic event. *Star Wars*, though not without sinister elements common to all science fiction, is an old time 'space opera'. The moral it draws may be opposed at many points to traditional spiritual doctrine, but still, for all its use of mythological themes provided by 'mythic advisor' Joseph Campbell, it is essentially an adventure story told for purposes of entertainment; it is not deliberate propaganda. *ET* is extremely suspect, particularly since it features a parody of Michelangelo's image in the Sistine Chapel of God creating Adam by touching his finger—it regularly produced a kind of maudlin, pseudo-religious reaction in people to whom all normal religious emotions were apparently foreign—but there is nothing in it that can't be explained by the generally-accepted anti-clericalism and aesthetic satanism endemic to Hollywood culture. *Close Encounters of the Third Kind*, on the other hand, with its exaltation of the psychopathic tendency prevalent in contemporary culture to cut all one's economic and emotional ties in the pursuit of some fantastic and empty ideal, is another matter; from the time it first came out I have always thought of it as a mind-control job. It is nothing less than a satanic counterfeit of the 'rapture': instead of sound doctrine and religious faith, in the context of the intense psychic and spiritual energies unleashed at the apocalyptic end of the aeon, leading to the ecstatic experience of the presence of God, it presents emotional nihilism, spiritual emptiness and the lack of any stable frame of reference as the prerequisites for a willing capitulation to inhuman forces—and presents this outcome as 'positive'. The 'hero' of the movie throws his entire life away to pursue the source of the sound in his head of a few musical notes and the mental image of a barren desert crag—experiences which various forms of hypnosis and mind-control may well be able to produce with the greatest of ease—and is rewarded by being willingly abducted by an alien spaceship. That many who viewed *Close Encounters* took it as much more than mere entertainment was demonstrated to me in the late '80s, when I attended a party at the house of New Age musician Constance Demby. A few notes of music had appeared mysteriously on one of her audio tapes! Our blithe and enthusiastic hostess played them for us, and interpreted them, not surprisingly, as a personal message from the Space Brothers, on the model of the musical notes in *Close Encounters*. It goes without saying that no one in the room contradicted her; one of the most effective methods of self-induced mind-control, as we all know, is based on fear of the social *faux-pas!* [Note: Not being a film buff, it was only after I finished writing this chapter that I realized that the three productions which seemed most like mind-control to me—*Close Encounters*, *ET*, and *Roswell*—were all produced by Steven Spielberg! No one, of course, should draw any hard conclusions from this; it may be that Mr Spielberg simply has a mind-control-like style of motion picture production.]

The 1994 TV 'docu-drama' *Roswell*, starring Martin Sheen, about the supposed crash of an alien spaceship in New Mexico in 1947, and the recovery both of alien corpses and of surviving aliens who later died, will serve as an even better example. Jacques Vallee, in *Revelations*, tells us why he believes it unlikely that the Roswell incident was the crash of an alien spacecraft. He also gives us an interesting piece of information which contradicts the TV version of the event. According to Vallee, the first people to reach the supposed crash site encountered another group already there, who described themselves as 'archaeologists'. Vallee speculates that their real role may have been to plant the mysterious material which was later claimed to be the debris of the spaceship—a material which, according to him, could easily have been produced by human technology as it existed in 1947. In *Roswell*, however, the statement is made that the object could not have been a crashed experimental aircraft because 'they'd be looking for it' if it were, but no one appeared; the site, when first approached after the incident, was deserted. Obviously these two statements do not add up.

Among the more common mind-control techniques, useful to anyone who wishes to use it and can command sufficient attention via the media or the internet, is the Government Coverup Ploy: if you assert that a given fact is true but that the government is covering it up, a certain percentage of the public will automatically believe you—especially if you can pressure the government to the point where it will start issuing denials. It's a cheap and reliable tool; even the government itself can use it. *Roswell* is based upon the Government Coverup Ploy, as are a number of even more obviously propagandistic 'documentaries' and 'leaks' relating to the Roswell incident which have subsequently appeared. But *Roswell* is also a good specimen of two much more sophisticated mind-control techniques, ones which must be classed as satanic, since they represent perversions of specific metaphysical principles. I have named these techniques *subliminal contradiction* and *deferred closure.*

In the words of Jacques Vallee,

> it is possible to make large sections of any population believe in the existence of supernatural races, in the possibility of flying machines, in the plurality of inhabited worlds, by exposing them to a few carefully engineered scenes, the details of which are adapted to the culture and superstitions of a particular time and place.[1]

Seraphim Rose comments that

> an important clue to the meaning of these 'engineered scenes' may be seen in the observation often made by careful observers of UFO phenomena, especially CE-III ['close encounters of the third kind', i.e., sightings of sentient 'aliens'] and 'contactee' cases: that they are profoundly 'absurd', or contain at least as much absurdity as reality. Individual 'Close Encounters' have absurd details, like the four pancakes given by a UFO occupant to a Wisconsin chicken farmer in 1961; more significantly, the encounters themselves are strangely pointless, without clear purpose or meaning. A Pennsylvania psychiatrist has suggested that the absurdity present in almost all UFO cases is actually a *hypnotic technique.* 'When the person is disturbed by the absurd or the contradictory, and their mind is searching for meaning, they are extremely open to thought transference, to receiving

1. *Passport to Magonia: From Folklore to Flying Saucers* (Chicago: Henry Regnery Co., 1969) pp150–1.

psychic healing, etc. ([Vallee] *The Invisible College* [E.P. Dutton], p115).[1]

Precisely. In the technique of subliminal contradiction, two mutually incompatible bits of information are simultaneously projected into the perception of the victim without the contradiction being either pointed out or explained. In the technique of deferred closure, inexplicable data are continually fed to the victim or victims over a period of time, data which always suggest the possibility of a rational explanation but never quite allow it. And since the human mind is designed to seek and produce both perceptual and rational closure, the mind subjected to deferred closure will react to the continued frustration of one of its most basic needs either by sinking into stunned exhaustion, or by producing a paranoid, delusional form of closure. Schizophrenia presents the mind with a flood of data which overwhelms the normal processes of emotional, rational and perceptual closure; paranoid schizophrenia represents a more or less successful attempt to reach relative closure by abnormal means. Deferred closure, then, might be defined as an experimental method for producing paranoid schizophrenia.[2]

Subliminal contradiction and deferred closure are not only mind-control techniques, however; they are also essential elements of postmodern 'philosophy', which believes that contradictory statements are not necessarily mutually exclusive, and that any closure as to the true nature of things, any 'overarching paradigm', is impossible. Postmodernism, both as a philosophy and as a name for our contemporary culture, employs subliminal contradiction and deferred closure simply because it can't imagine anything else; it no longer believes in the existence of objective truth. (This, in itself, is enough to explain 'the Spielberg Agenda', though not to absolutely disprove the existence of a more deliberate attempt at 'social engineering'.)

In *Messengers of Deception* we are introduced to UFO contactee

1. *Orthodoxy and the Religion of the Future*, p130.

2. For a fictional description of this technique, see *That Hideous Strength: A Modern Fairy-tale for Grown-ups* (New York: Macmillan, 1968), pp297–298).

Rael (Claude Vorilhon, whose patronymic subsequently appeared on the TV sci-fi series *Babylon 5* as the name of an alien race, the Vorilhons), a robed and bearded false prophet who wears a medallion based on a design supposedly shown him by the aliens. The design—a combination between a swastika and a star of David—is an instance of subliminal contradiction. And since the contradiction is addressed to the 'right brain' in the form of an image, rather than to the 'left brain' in the form of a statement, it is more likely to be accepted uncritically, since the role of the right cerebral hemisphere is to synthesize data, not analyze it. As soon as a subliminal contradiction is accepted into the field of perception without initial resistance, the critical faculty is stunned, and the mind becomes receptive to suggestion.

I wonder if anyone besides myself has seen the subliminal contradiction ploy as it operates in normal social situations. If a person who wishes to influence you can establish a clear image in your mind of who he is and what is to be expected of him, and then, swiftly and nonchalantly, say or do something which totally contradicts this image, without exhibiting the normal mischievousness or social anxiety which such a shift usually entails, you may accept both your image of him and its contrary simultaneously, and subliminally. If you do, he has stunned you into a state where you can easily be manipulated. A subliminal contradiction between speech and body language can have the same effect.

The UFO phenomenon as a whole, and the crop-circle phenomenon as well, is a case of the deferred closure technique. Are UFOs spaceships? Psychic entities? Human deceptions? Are they wise philosophers come to aid us, or sinister invaders here to destroy us? The ambiguity of the phenomenon in itself produces a state of deferred closure, but it is clear from Dr Vallee's researches that this ambiguity is also being deliberately exploited by human groups. If you put a person in a prison cell along with a sledgehammer, a Barbie Doll, a can of olives and a ball of copper wire, and tell him you'll let him out again as soon as he invents a philosophical system based on these four 'principles', he may astound you with his ability to make 'closure' on the intrinsic meanings of and inter-relationships between elements which, in any objective sense, do not allow for it.

His 'system' will say much more about his own deepest hopes, fears, beliefs and root assumptions than it will about the data you've provided him. And once you know what his 'system' is, then you can stress him further by feeding him data which again contradict it, ruining his meticulously-constructed pattern. Even better, you can feed him data which triumphantly confirm it—and onto which are grafted other items of information which you want him to accept as implicitly true. And he *will* accept them, because he experiences them not as alien beliefs which are being forced upon him against his will, but as parts of a pattern which *he himself has created*, through his own labor, imagination, sacrifice, and quest for truth.

Roswell is filled with subliminal contradictions, and the entire plot is an example of deferred closure. It is the story of Jesse Marcel, an Air Force officer who visits the crash site and picks up some of the mysterious material of which the craft was supposedly constructed—and later, in the course of a government coverup of the incident, is forced to lie about his experience. Jesse is the archetypal misunderstood paranoid crank, with whom many Americans can identify—but *we* the omniscient observers know he's telling the truth. We see him years later at a reunion of his old outfit, dying of emphysema. He's still determined to expose the coverup and get to the bottom of what really happened. He runs into a few others who had something to do with the incident, and hears the story about the recovery of alien bodies, and one live occupant. As the stories are told, we see flashbacks to 1947, some supposedly authentic, some only dramatizations of rumors. There is no resolution. Finally the mysterious UFO researcher and/or government and/or anti-government agent, Townsend (the Martin Sheen character) approaches Jesse and tells him more about the bizarre intricacies of the UFO phenomenon than he ever knew—referring, in the process, to *Close Encounters of the Third Kind*, the one other UFO film, except possibly *ET*, I picked out as a mind-control experiment—but leaves him as oppressed and puzzled as ever. Townsend has no final conclusions either, but nonetheless remains mysteriously knowledgeable and intimidating; after meeting with him, Jesse sinks into despair.

Whenever the incident is described, contradictory accounts are given. The alien bodies are smooth-skinned/no, their skin is scaly; their heads are egg-shaped/no, they are pear-shaped; the crashed object is flat and crescent- shaped (we see a quick flash of it)/no, it is egg-shaped (we see a quick contradictory flash); the name of the mortician who was contacted by the Air Force is Paul Davis/no, David Paulus. The bodies number five or six/no, three or four; the bodies are human-like/no, child-like (as if children aren't human)/ no, foetus-like; the ship is cylindrical/no, round/no, egg-shaped/ no, dome-shaped: the disorienting patter goes on and on. At one point we are shown a newspaper headline from the *Roswell Daily Record* reporting on the official debunking of the incident as a crashed weather balloon: *'Gen. Ramey Empties Roswell Saucer.'* This, on the face of it, means little or nothing, unless it is a bad pun on the act of pouring out spilled tea. Subliminally, it means two different and contradictory things: That the general 'empties' the incident of meaning—i.e., calls it unreal—and that he *unloads* the saucer itself, indicating that it is a real object out of which real things can be taken, presumably the alien bodies. Since this is apparently an actual headline of the time, we can't attribute the subliminal contradiction it contains to Steven Spielberg. So how can we explain it? Elaborate conspiracy theories aside—such as the involvement of the intelligence community in all aspects of the Roswell incident from day one—perhaps someone on the staff of the *Roswell Daily Record* who believed in the crash constructed the headline so as to debunk the official debunkers. Or it may simply represent—and this in no way invalidates the above explanations—the intuitive reaction of the human mind, on a deeply unconscious level, to 'archetypal idea' of the UFO as a 'messenger of deception'.

The action is repeatedly intercut with religious imagery. When Jesse first shows the mysterious saucer-material to his family, it appears below a picture of Jesus on the wall of his home. When Townsend makes his mysterious and mystifying revelations to Jesse, the scene begins with a priest giving a memorial service for deceased fliers outside a hangar; Townsend takes Jesse inside the hangar, tells him the UFO secrets, then leaves. At the end, we return to the memorial service and the priest. The scene is designed to give the distinct though subliminal impression that the Catholic service is the outer or exoteric form, *and the UFO-lore the inner or esoteric meaning.* The themes of the sacred *temenos*, temple or mystery-cave, and the initiatory experience as a spiritual death (the memorial service) are also exploited— but not a death and *rebirth*, since Jesse remains inside the hanger and never re-emerges, in that scene, into the sunlight. The suggestion is that the UFO phenomenon is equivalent to, and will replace, revealed religion—a suggestion made more explicit in the scene where the Air Force brass assigned to investigate the incident repeat the belief that 'aliens' have manipulated human genetics and inspired human religious leaders throughout history, and are told by their superior, 'Think of our religious institutions if all of this were to just come out, what are people going to believe in?' and the scene where Jesse's son tells his dying father, who believes he's close to discovering the truth, 'You're close to nothing. Face it, Dad, you're never going to find what you're looking for, you just want an answer like there's some proof out there of God, or an afterlife, UFOs, it's all the same thing, something to hang onto when nothing makes sense, this is fantasy, to make you feel better in the night.' So in the face of death, that 'nothing', that 'night', no faith is permitted; knock, and no door will be opened.

But the real goal of *Roswell* and other UFO-related propaganda is revealed in the scene where an officer participating in the investigation is shown in a picture gallery, looking up (briefly, so as to set up a 'waking suggestion') at perhaps an 18th or 19th century portrait of a haloed 'saint', who is gazing upward and to his right at a light-beam suggestive of God's glory—or a beam from a UFO—but holding in his left hand a red object emitting white flames, flames which are actually kindling his halo; the object appears to be the head of a demon. The officer is asking: 'Under what agency will we be operating?' His colleague answers him, 'None, we will have complete control.' Here we can begin to see the meaning of the tradition that Satan has saints and contemplatives of his own, who answer to neither God nor man. On the other hand, the saint is *under* the light-beam in the painting, just as the officer is under the painting itself; word and image and directly contradictory on a subliminal level. And the fact that the saint holds the demon's fiery head—if that's what it is—in his hand, shows that he is in control of it, or believes he is, much as the ceremonial magician of the Renaissance would invoke the power of God, or one of His angels, to give him control over the demon he wished to enslave. Here the desire for Promethean spiritual autonomy is used to deny the truth that the sorcerer, even though he clearly worships his own self-will as if it were God, is in fact handing that will over to the control of an infernal will by that very worship. This is the 'denial'—and also the 'co-dependency'—which affects all magicians: self-determination is enslavement, but every worshipper of self-determination must deny this, until it is too late.

Roswell also does what it can to muddle and neutralize the findings of honest researchers like Vallee. When the military big-wigs are discussing how to cover up the Roswell crash, one asks 'what if people think we are not in control of the skies?' and another answers 'they'd be right'—thus setting up another subliminal contradiction to 'we're in complete control.' Then they propose that 'hoaxes' be carried out, and that true information be leaked through unreliable and suspect sources as part of the coverup. But why hoaxes? How can a convincingly staged UFO appearance or landing convince people that there are no such things as UFOs? It can do so only if it is later proved to be a hoax—but that is the one thing which is almost never absolutely provable when UFO deceptions are alleged. All that Vallee has been able to come up with are tantalizing clues that a particular manifestation could have been a deception, and evidence convincing enough to suggest that the phenomenon as a whole includes deception activities by human groups. But if anything is clear in this murky world, it is that whatever deceptions are being carried on are meant to be believed, not to be disproved. As for leaking of true information via untrustworthy sources, that *is* being done, in order to set up a 'feedback loop' between lunatic cranks and cynical debunkers. But the purpose of such a loop, according to Vallee in *Messengers of Deception*, is to discourage objective investigation of the phenomenon, *not* to convince people that there are no such things as UFOs. If that were its purpose, one would have to conclude that it is not a very effective strategy, given that every time someone who has investigated the actual data, or has himself experienced the phenomenon, hears it cynically debunked by the 'authorities', academic or military, those authorities lose more credibility in his eyes—and every time that person or someone like him voices his or her legitimate feeling that the authorities are either deluded or dishonest in regard to the phenomenon, the officials in question become even more cynical and self-defensive, and so lose that much more *authority* over those upon whose trust they depend. And into that vacuum of social and cultural authority come—the UFOs. Jacques Vallee believes that this method of discouraging objective investigation is largely for the purpose of hiding the activities of human groups, possibly allowing them to test new high-tech weapons, or 'psychotronic' devices for the manipulation of human consciousness, without public or political interference. I agree. But there are other reasons for it. This lowering of collective consciousness and diminishment of our sense of reality is being deliberately engineered for two purposes: first, in order to make the public more suggestible and open to a belief in UFOs, and secondly to lull us into a false sense of 'security'—really a psychic numbness based on repressed fear—so that we will not realize that UFOs represent a mass psychic invasion of the most alarming nature, requiring an immediate and militant response on the plane of spiritual warfare. This *abaissement de niveau mental* is served by a number of devices, not the least of which is the tendency to portray aliens in comic mode, which completes the triad of Fear/Worship/Complacency that can be seen around other horrendous possibilities—that of human cloning, for example. We fear them; we laugh at them in order to deny our fear; as soon as our fear is suppressed, we accept them. This engineered unreality is symbolized in *Roswell* by the alcoholic haze in which the stories of the UFO crash are exchanged at the Air Force reunion; one of the informants, sluggish and overweight, appears floating on his back in a swimming pool with a drink on his belly. It's not an image designed to promote either critical awareness or spiritual vigilance.

The central intent of the writers and producers of *Roswell* surfaces in the scene where Townsend is 'educating' Jesse Marcel in the hangar; the following is an excerpt from their dialogue:

> Townsend: One must proceed cautiously here, on guard against one's desire to want it to be true or want it not to be true. One must be, as much as possible, neutral.
>
> Jesse Marcel: Well, how can you be neutral? A thing is either true or it's not, there is no middle ground.
>
> T: Alright, alright . . . then none of it is true.
>
> J: *None* of it?
>
> T: Well, maybe some of it. . .
>
> J: No, no, you're playing with me—why are you playing with me?
>
> T: Because maybe you wouldn't even know what was true if you'd seen it all for yourself. How's that for an answer?
>
> J: Alright, then what did I see out there in that field?
>
> T: That? . . . why, that was a weather balloon.
>
> J: *No*, it wasn't, I know what I saw, and it was not from this world.
>
> T: Don't you understand, Jesse, you have *nothing*, just a lot of old memories and second hand recollections. Nobody is going to take you seriously, not without proof, not without hard evidence.

What is being preached here is nothing less that the impossibility of arriving at objective truth, and ultimately the unreality of objective truth itself. Irreducible subjectivities, with no overarching paradigm to unite them into an integrated vision of reality, are all we have—all we are. It is the whole postmodern age and postmodernist agenda in a nutshell; and since objective Truth is ultimately God, what is being preached is also a denial of God, and His replacement by demonic principalities and powers. But without grounding in the Divine objectivity of the Ground of Being, even our ability to draw rational conclusions from empirical data becomes eroded, since rationality is nothing less than a distant mental echo of Intellection, or Divine Gnosis. In the words of C.S. Lewis from *That Hideous Strength* (1946), his science fiction novel about an invasion of Earth by the forces of the Antichrist (which I heard Traditionalist author James Cutsinger describe as '*The Reign of Quantity* in fictional form'):

> The physical sciences, good and innocent in themselves, had already . . . begun to be warped, had been subtly maneuvered in a certain direction. Despair of objective truth had been increasingly insinuated into the scientists; indifference to it, and a concentration upon mere power, had been the result. Babble about the *élan vital* and flirtations with panpsychism were bidding fair to restore the *Anima Mundi* of the magicians. . . . The very experiences of the dissecting room and the pathological laboratory were breeding a conviction that a stifling of all deep-set repugnances was the first essential for progress. [p 203]

The heart of the matter—which appears in the first two passages of the above dialogue—is a *deliberate* and *engineered* attack upon the concept of objective truth; the postmodernist deconstructionism of academia is nothing but the stifling vapor rising up from a much deeper and darker cauldron. When Townsend says that we must be on guard against *wanting* the extraterrestrial hypothesis to be true or not true, he is accurately presenting one of the prerequisites for real objectivity—then, instead of the word 'objective', he uses the word *neutral*. But neutrality is not necessarily objectivity; it can just as easily denote nihilism or indifference. And Jesse senses this nihilism, which is what leads him to reject the stance of neutrality, to protest that 'A thing is either true or it's not, there's no middle ground.' But as Townsend has set things up, Jesse defeats himself by this very protest, since *he has been manoeuvred into defending objectivity by attacking the very criteria of objectivity*, which have falsely been associated with a nihilistic neutrality—a neutrality which, in this context, is really nothing but another name for 'suggestibility'. How ingenious, how cunning the writers and producer (Steven Spielberg) of *Roswell* were, and are. But if they're so smart, one is led to ask, then why can't they be intelligent? Because that would not be in the interest of the forces they consciously or unconsciously serve; all intelligence is of God.

A truly inverted and satanic *metaphysics* is at the origin of *Roswell*. Subliminal contradiction is a satanic counterfeit of the metaphysical principle that the Absolute is beyond the 'symplegades', the pairs-of-opposites. Deferred closure is a satanic counterfeit of the metaphysical principle that the Infinite cannot, by definition, be contained within any system of thought or perception. Absoluteness and Infinity, according to the metaphysics of Frithjof Schuon, are properly descriptive of the Divine Essence of God, and nothing else. To apply them to anything relative and contingent, anything in the realm of cosmic manifestation, is the highest form of idolatry, perhaps best characterized as a deception of 'Iblis', the Muslim name for Satan, or the satanic principle, in its most metaphysically subtle mode of action. The Absolute, or Necessary Being, is not realized through an amalgamation or confusion of the pairs of opposites, but through transcendence of them, after which it is seen exactly how the Absolute manifests by means of them. And the Infinite, or Possible Being, is not realized through a foredoomed attempt to reduce the Infinite Possibility within the Divine Nature to a closed system, but simply through accepting what comes and letting go of what must go, in the knowledge that all things are a manifestation of God's will, either in terms of what He positively wills—Being, or the good—and what He negatively allows—the privation of Being, or evil—in view of the fact that universe, though it manifests Him, is not He Himself, and is thus necessarily imperfect. Submission to God's will as manifest in the events of our lives—a submission which does not exclude, but actually requires, our creative response to these events, since our innate desire to live shapely and fully-realized lives is also part of God's will—leads to the gnosis of all events as acts of God, which opens in turn on the deeper gnosis of all manifest forms as eternal, archetypal possibilities within the embrace of the Divine Infinity. The realization of God as Infinite is not the desire for an ultimate philosophical or experiential closure but the sacrifice of this desire in the face of the Divine Immanence; the realization of God as Absolute is not the horizontal confusion or neutralization of polarities, but the vertical intuition of their common Principle in the light of the Divine Transcendence.

In the last scene, we see Jesse Marcel hopelessly puttering around the crash site in the dry autumn grass, looking for 'hard evidence'—

remnants of the UFO crash debris which were all collected 30 years ago. He is seeking for certainty not where it can really be found, in the objective Ground of Being, but precisely where it can never be found: in memory. Jesse, his wife and his son come together again as a family around a sense of a bleak, nostalgic futility: 'We can never know the truth,' the movie says, 'but at least we can huddle together emotionally on the basis of a common despair of knowing it.' And so *Roswell* ends with one more satanic counterfeit: that of *humility*. Instead of a pious awe in the face of what transcends form, we are left with a stunned, mesmerized hopelessness in the face of what has never reached it, or has fallen below it. Nonetheless, as Rumi says, counterfeit coins only exist because there really is such a thing as true gold; or, in the words of Meister Eckhart, 'The more he blasphemes, the more he praises God.' So the spiritual practice, here, is not to struggle with the shadows of contradiction and uncertainty, but to turn 180 degrees away from them. It is to let the counterfeit remind you of the Truth: to make hopeless contradiction a way of remembering the Absolute Divine Truth which eternally possesses the power to resolve it, and endless uncertainty a way of remembering the Infinite Divine Life which radiates from the core of that Truth, by which we can, in Blake's famous words,

see the world in a grain of sand
And Heaven in a wild flower
... hold Infinity in the palm of your hand
And Eternity in an hour.

False humility before what is less real than you are makes you arrogant, and destroys your human dignity. True humility before what is infinitely greater than you are blesses and uplifts you, which is why Muslims say that man, *because* he is God's slave, is thereby His vicegerent, His fully-empowered representative in this world.

ABDUCTION: THE ONTOLOGICAL AGENDA

Alien contact represents an irruption into the material plane of subhuman forces from the subtle realm, whose goal is the dissolution of our world. But though dissolution is the natural end of any cycle of manifestation, we aren't required to capitulate to the forces which produce it, because there is a spark of the Divine Nature within us which is beyond manifestation entirely, which was not veiled by its beginning nor corrupted by its fall, and will not be altered by its end. But if we forget this, if we turn our spiritual attention away from the Spirit of God and toward the forces of chaos and subversion which are It's shadow, then our return to Him—which, according to the Qur'an, is the destiny of all beings—will be indefinitely delayed, and will ultimately take place by the dark road of infernal torment, not the road of God's Mercy, the path of Divine Love and Wisdom.

According to René Guénon, as you'll remember, the adoption of materialistic beliefs by the mass of mankind resulted in an actual 'solidification of the world'. But materialism has already moved past its apex, a truth which Guénon saw in 1945, and which is much more obvious today. In the late 19th century, when materialist ideology was at its strongest, both religion and 'superstition' were debunked. But today, as this ideology continues to lose power—the fall of the Soviet Union being one of the clearest signs of this—and as a belief in subtle beings and invisible worlds becomes more acceptable, such acceptance does not take the form of a return to religion and metaphysics, which continue to be eroded, but rather that of a collective fascination with mysterious and sinister possibilities, exactly as Guénon predicted. The post-modern 'transcendence' of the modernist paradigm, to which materialism was integral—Marx and Darwin being two of modernism's central pillars—has resulted not in a renaissance of traditional theology but in a nihilistic worship of fragmentation and chaos in the name of the 'celebration of diversity'. Postmodernism shows itself to be a toxic stew in which arcane science, disintegrated cultural material and 'infra-psychic' forces are mixed in relatively equal amounts. In Guénon's own words:

> the materialistic conception, once it has been formed and spread abroad in one way or another, can only serve to reinforce the very 'solidification' of the world that in the first place made it possible . . . the 'solidification' . . . can never be complete, and there are limits beyond which it cannot go . . . the farther 'solidification' goes the more precarious it becomes, for the lowest degree is also the least stable; the ever-growing rapidity of the changes taking place in the world today provides all-too-eloquent testimony to the truth of this . . . though the hold of materialism is slackening, there is no occasion to rejoice in the fact, for cyclical manifestation is not yet complete, and the 'fissures' . . . can only be produced from below; in other words, that which 'interferes' with the sensible world through those 'fissures' can be nothing but an inferior 'cosmic psychism' in its most destructive and disorganizing forms, and it is moreover clear that influences of this kind are the only ones that are really suited for action having dissolution as its objective . . . , everything that tends to favor and extend these 'interferences' merely corresponds, whether consciously or otherwise, to a fresh phase of the deviation of which materialism in reality represented a less 'advanced' stage. . . . In the Islamic tradition these 'fissures' are those by which, at the end of the cycle, the devastating hordes of Gog and Magog will force their way in, for they are unremitting in their efforts to invade this world; these 'entities' represent the inferior influences in question.[1]

No clearer presentation of the 'ontological agenda' of today's 'aliens' is available to us than the book entitled *Abduction: Human Encounters with Aliens*, by Pulitzer Prize-winning author and Harvard psychiatrist John E. Mack. Based on nearly one hundred cases of 'alien abduction', Dr Mack (like Jacques Vallee, whose preeminence as a UFOlogist Mack affirms) concludes that such abductions are real, and that they are carried on by entities from subtler planes of being who have the power to physically impinge upon this one. He delves more deeply than Dr Vallee into the ongoing psychological and

1. *The Reign of Quantity*, pp145, 147, 202, 206.

psycho-physical 'covenant' which is often established between aliens and their abductees, but ignores, for some reason, Vallee's findings about the involvement of human groups practicing deception and mind-control.

According to Mack, alien abduction seems to run in families. Many abductees had alcoholic or emotionally frigid parents, came from broken homes, or suffered childhood sexual abuse. Mack mentions one study in which the abduction experience is related to ritual abuse by Satanic cults. Interaction with 'aliens' can begin as early as the age of 2 or 3. In childhood they often appear as relatively benign, but when the abductee reaches puberty their actions become more sinister. Abductees sometimes transfer to the aliens feelings of love which were not reciprocated in the family setting, and experience being loved in return. Many abductees, in Mack's estimation, seem particularly psychic or intuitive; many experience the development of psychic powers as a result of the abduction itself.

The 'aliens' exhibit characteristics commonly encountered in shamanism; they, or their craft, sometimes appear as animals. They also bear an obvious resemblance to traditional 'gods, spirits, angels, fairies, demons, ghouls, vampires and sea monsters'—though it appears that Mack is incapable of differentiating between the various types of subtle beings, or doesn't want to. And though UFO sightings are a world-wide occurrence, most abductions are reported from the Western hemisphere, with the United States heading the list.

(The correlation of UFO activity with emotional frigidity has an interesting sidelight: Breakaway Freudian psychoanalyst Wilhelm Reich, the father of much of today's 'bodywork', was attempting toward the end of his life—when many believe he had become mentally imbalanced—to manipulate and enhance a subtle 'life-energy' which he named 'orgone', as part of his struggle against the 'emotional plague'. This was his name for a *mass freezing of human emotion*, often expressed in terms of what he called 'character armor', as well as through social movements such as Nazism. According to Reich, UFOs, as a source of 'deadly orgone energy', were in part responsible for this plague.)

The alien abductors subject their victims to terrifying and humiliating 'medical-like' procedures. They also voyeuristically view them performing sexual intercourse, or themselves have intercourse with them. One of the major agendas of the aliens seems to be to extract human sperm and egg cells from their abductees so as to genetically engineer a 'hybrid' human/ alien race. Female abductees experience these hybrid fetuses being placed in their womb, then somehow removed a few months later, to continue their growth aboard alien 'spacecraft'.

Their 'mothers' are sometimes re-abducted, and then directed to show mother-love to these hybrid beings, who appear 'listless'. *No evidence exists of actual physical pregnancies.* After abduction, many victims experience themselves as now possessing, or as always having possessed, a dual 'human/alien' identity; they sometimes see themselves as performing the same 'procedures' or 'experiments' upon new abductees as were originally performed upon them.

Among the case histories Dr Mack presents are some of the most horrifying stories of demonic attack and possession I have ever encountered, though he does not recognize them as such. He admits (p13) that 'Abductees . . . bear physical and psychological scars of their experience. These range from nightmares and anxiety to chronic nervous agitation, depression, even psychosis, to actual physical scars—puncture and incision marks, scrapes, burns and sores.' He speaks of broken marriages and alienation of affection between parents and children as among the more common aftereffects, and says that negative physical and psychological effects persist even in cases where spontaneous healing of chronic or incurable diseases occurs. One would naturally assume, therefore, that his therapeutic approach would include an attempt to shield his patients from ongoing alien influence, and help them break any psychological ties which might remain. But this is not in fact the case, because Mack, appallingly, believes that the influence of the aliens, by and large, is good! He views his role as one of helping his clients to remember their abduction experiences, often via hypnosis (which, incidentally, has been proved so unreliable as a tool for accessing 'recovered memories' that the courts have disallowed testimony based upon it)—and then helping them to deal with the violent and horrific emotions such memories entail—*and then helping them to accept that their experience is (somehow) ultimately 'positive', 'transformative', or 'spiritual'.* He sees himself as supporting them more against skeptical therapists and family members than against the alien kidnappers themselves. 'In my work with abductees,' he says, 'I am fully involved, experiencing and reliving with them [*sic*] the world that they are calling forth from their unconscious.' One gets the distinct impression that the therapeutic session with Dr Mack is actually the missing second half of the abduction experience itself, which includes both an original deeply traumatic event or series of events, and the eventual acceptance of the experience, *in contradiction to all the patient's deepest feelings*, as a 'message' or 'mission' from the aliens, in the 'permissive', 'supportive', 'non-threatening', 'non-judgmental, 'accepting' therapeutic framework provided by Dr Mack. It would be interesting, however, to see how some of Mack's patients would react in a different environment—that of a traditional exorcism, for example. Would their deliberately suppressed feelings of being profoundly violated reassert themselves in such a context? Would the full acceptance of these feelings lead to a radically different conclusion about the aliens' true agenda? Mack himself seems to view his interaction with his clients as part of the 'composition' of the abduction experience. He describes it as a 'co-creative' process, 'the product of an intermingling of flowing-together of the consciousness of two (or more) people in the room. Something may be brought forth that was not there before in exactly the same form' (p391). Precisely.

Reading Mack is like watching, through a two-way mirror, the putterings of a confused physician who is so fascinated by the task of diagnosing a disease that he has forgotten that it is his duty to heal his patient. Perhaps he simply doesn't know how to begin to treat the disease which confronts him. But one can only conclude from his book—since he comes right out and says it—that he accepts the alien agenda reported by his tormented and traumatized patients, *because they themselves accept it.* Is this the final form of the 'client-centered therapy' of Carl Rogers? The idea that, since the patient has chosen schizophrenia, or demonic possession, the role of the psychiatrist is to support him in this choice, and help him go crazy? *Of course* the client 'accepts' the alien program: he is possessed by it, precisely as a human cell invaded by a virus, which utilizes the cell's own genetic structure to create replicas of itself, is possessed by the virus. But just because a person's immune system fails to overcome the attack of a microbe, do we therefore second it in its 'choice'? Is this good medical practice? (Not for nothing did C.S. Lewis, in *That Hideous Strength*, call the demonic space-beings and/or fallen angels battling to conquer Earth the 'macrobes'.) Mack casts about for scattered fragments of spiritual and occult lore to explain what his patients are going through, and comes up with little more than evidence that such things have always occurred, coupled with speculations based upon the statements made by the aliens themselves! But if someone kidnaps and tortures me, is that any indication that I ought to believe what he says? Is such an attitude in any way rational, not to mention sound on the level of normal human emotion? And the fact that similar things have occurred throughout history is purely elementary. The power of realities from unseen dimensions to impinge on our world has always been part of human knowledge, its suppression by reductionist materialism over the past couple of centuries notwithstanding. Mack builds his case for accepting the alien agenda on the fact that their very presence overturns the materialist paradigm. But if so, then why can't he accept the common consensus of the pre-materialist millennia, when it was well understood—as it still is by many today—that manifestations such as he reports indicate the presence of demons, and that demons are, in every case where it serves their ends—and sometimes because they simply can't help themselves—deliberate liars? He gleefully profits from materialism's denial of the validity of religion and of any sense of moral order in the universe; it is precisely what allows him to accept a purely demonic reality of a subtle nature—coupled with a sinister and self-contradictory philosophy—and then introduce it as the herald of a major paradigm-shift *because it transcends materialism*. This is exactly what Guénon meant when he said that materialism first 'solidifies' the human mindset, and then produces 'fissures' opening not on the 'celestial' but on the 'infra-psychic'.

The correct practice when confronted with such manifestations as alien abduction, for which the hard evidence continues to mount, is simply to admit the obvious, that such manifestations exist, and then proceed to ask the questions which will immediately occur to any normal, religiously-educated human being: (1) Is the manifestation in question good, neutral, or evil? (2) If it is good, what does it ask of us? (3) If it is neutral, is it useful or a waste of time? (4) If it is evil, how can we avoid and/or combat it? Someone who cannot ask even these most elementary and inevitable of questions is in no way a physician of souls. And, unfortunately, Mack falls into this category. He seems to believe that to ask moral questions about what appear to be the deliberate actions of conscious beings is somehow unscientific, and repeats the common nihilist cliché, derived from a counterfeit metaphysics, that beings from subtler planes are in some way beyond good and evil. He ignorantly attributes this counterfeit metaphysics to Tibetan Buddhism, and opposes it to that of Judeo-Christianity:

> To the polarizing perception of Christian dualism these dark-eyed beings seem to be the playmates of the Devil (Downing, 1990). Eastern religious traditions such as Tibetan Buddhism, which have always recognized the vast range of spirit entities in the cosmos, seem to have less difficulty accepting the actuality of the UFO abduction phenomenon than do the more dualistic monotheisms, which offer powerful resistance to acceptance.[1]

In relation to the belief that higher realities are morally neutral, Frithjof Schuon's teaching on the subject is as follows: God may be 'beyond good and evil' because He transcends all relativity, but this does not mean that He is 'beyond good', or morally neutral in His relation to us, or somehow half good and half evil. He is the Sovereign Good, beyond any conceivable relationship with the fragmentary and privative manifestation we call 'evil'. His goodness transcends definition as 'the opposite of evil' not because it is in any way involved with evil, but because it is Absolute, and consequently has no opposite.

When Mack uses the word 'acceptance' in the above passage, does he mean 'acceptance as real' or 'acceptance as good and/or inevitable,'

1. New York: Scribner's, 1994, p412.

as when he helps his clients in the therapeutic setting to overcome their natural resistance and *accept* the alien agenda? He seems to be saying that Tibetan Buddhism, with its understanding of 'the vast range of spirit entities in the cosmos,' accepts them as real, whereas the Christian tradition does not. But Christianity, in seeing the aliens as 'playmates of the Devil', obviously does accept them as real, by Mack's own admission. Mack makes the word 'acceptance' deliberately ambiguous in order to imply that, while Christianity narrow-mindedly rejects the aliens as evil, broad-minded Tibetan Buddhism accepts them as a natural part of the cosmos; but all he has really been able to factually assert is that the Tibetan Buddhists believe they are real—which, of course, is also true of the Christians. His obvious intent is to drive a wedge between Christianity and Buddhism, and to imply that the Tibetans, in accepting aliens as real, necessarily accept them as good, as if Tibetan Buddhism possessed no doctrine of the demonic. Such, of course, is not the case. Both Christianity and the Vajrayana recognize the existence of demonic entities, the difference being that Christians believe they are eternally damned, while Buddhists hold that after their karmic debts are paid they can move on to relatively less infernal modes of existence, and that great saints can, on occasion, even convert them to Buddhism! But their profoundly destructive effects, and the need to vigorously combat them spiritually, are fully recognized by both traditions; to imply the contrary is either culpably ignorant or effectively slanderous to Tibetan Buddhism. And just because demons are esoterically understood in the Vajrayana as apparitions conceived in one's own mind, which symbolize obscuring attachments and passions, in no way makes them less real; after all, the human form itself is also an apparition conceived in one's own mind—which is ultimately the mind of the Buddha—symbolic in this case of the 'human state hard-to- attain', the only state from which the potential for Perfect Total Enlightenment can be realized.

Padma-sambhava, the great Vajrayana adept who brought Buddhism to Tibet, spent a lot his time combatting and subjugating demons. The following passages are from *The Tibetan Book of the Great Liberation* by W.Y. Evans- Wentz:

> Then Padma thought: 'I cannot very well spread the Doctrine and aid sentient beings until I destroy evil' . . . he subjugated all . . . demons and evil spirits, slew them, and took their hearts and blood into his mouth. Their consciousness-principles he transmuted into the syllable *Hum* and caused the *Hum* to vanish into the heaven-worlds. . . . Transforming himself into the King of the Wrathful Deities, Padma, while sitting in meditation, subjugated the Gnomes. . . . Padma performed magical dances on the surface of a boiling poisonous lake, and all the malignant and demoniacal *nagas* inhabiting the lake made submission to him . . . he subjugated various kinds of demons, such as those causing epidemics, diseases, hindrances, hail, and famine. . . . Padma brought all the gods inhabiting the heavens presided over by Brahma under his control. . . . And, in other guises, Padma conquered all the most furious and fearful evil spirits, and 21,000 devils, male and female . . . the goddesses Remati and Ekadzati appeared before Padma and praised him for thus having conquered all evils and all deities[1].

In line with Mack's findings, the aliens should obviously be classed among the 'demons causing diseases and hindrances'—but if he is so respectful of Tibetan Buddhism, why doesn't he see them as forces to be subjugated? I assume it is because he is no more a Vajrayana Buddhist than he is a Christian, though he feels no shame at taking the doctrines of both traditions out of context, and using them for his own ends. 'There can be little place,' he says, 'especially within the Judeo-Christian tradition, for a variety of small but powerful homely beings who administer an odd mixture of trauma and transcendence without apparent regard for any established religious hierarchy or doctrine' (p412). But, as we have just seen, Judeo-Christianity has a perfect place for them: the infernal regions. Their lack of 'regard' for any 'established religious hierarchy or doctrine' clearly does not represent an inability on the part of the revealed religions to make sense of them, but rather a will on the aliens' part to discredit the revealed religions—an agenda which

1. London: Oxford University Press, 1968; pp139–142.

Mack, as demonstrated in the above passage, supports. And there is no better way to undermine revealed religion than by associating the idea of 'transcendence' with the idea of 'traumatic violation', thus separating the True from the Good in the victims' minds, and associating Truth, not with Goodness, but with evil, and naked power (thereby also, by implication, making the Good appear weak). According to traditional metaphysics, pure Being is in itself the Sovereign Good whom we call God; consequently the more real something is the better it is, and the better something is the more real it is. It is the goal of the Antichrist to separate Truth from Goodness and Love, and unite it instead with ruthless power, so as to wipe Goodness and Love from the earth.

Mack repeatedly answers critics who attribute the abductees' acceptance of the aliens' agenda to the 'Stockholm Syndrome', the documented psychological tendency of victims to identify with their tormentors, as Patty Hearst did with the terrorists who kidnapped her. He says:

> In contrast to the narrow and self-serving purposes of human abusers and political kidnappers, the beings reveal a shared purpose, and offer the possibility of opening to an inclusive, more expansive worldview that is powerfully internalized by many abductees. (p339)

But Patty Hearst was also opened to a 'shared purpose' based on an 'inclusive, more expansive worldview,' that of global class struggle as opposed to the sheltered life of a rich and spoiled playgirl, by the Simbionese Liberation Army; and any child whose first sexual experience is with an abductor or molester has certainly had his or her worldview widened, though in a terribly destructive manner. There is no necessary contradiction between a 'self-serving purpose' and a 'more expansive worldview'. Hitler, who was not only self-serving but made the act of serving him into a pseudo-religion, opened some extremely expansive vistas to the German people. Unfortunately for them, and for the rest of the world, they were vistas of evil.

On p407, Dr Mack attempts to *defend humiliating and dehumanizing abuse* as a positive and transformative experience. He says:

> I am often asked how experiences that are so traumatic, and even cruel at times, can also be spiritually transformative. To me there is no inconsistency here, unless one reserves spirituality for realms that are free of pain and struggle. Sometimes our most useful spiritual learning comes at the hands of rough teachers who have little respect for our conceits, psychological defenses, or established points of view.

Whatever his intent, such a sweeping statement might be construed as a defense, not only of the 'right' of aliens to abduct us, but of the 'right' of megalo-maniac gurus and unethical psychiatrists *to psychologically and sexually abuse their devotees and clients.* It is true that the Nazi death-camp experience was powerfully transformative in a spiritual sense for some Jews; Elie Wiesel and Victor Frankl come immediately to mind. But does this mean that the Nazis were a spiritual force for good in the world? In the words of Jesus of Nazareth: 'There needs be evil, but woe to him through whom evil comes.' Whether one believes in UFOs and alien abduction or not, the grave dangers of Mack's approach should be obvious.

Incredibly, Mack sees the abduction experience as a paradigm of 'personal growth and transformation.' On pp 48–49 he presents it in terms of eight elements, or stages:

(1) Pushing through ego-death to acceptance;

(2) Recognizing the aliens as intermediaries between the human state and an impersonal cosmic consciousness;

(3) Experiencing ecstatic return 'Home' to this consciousness;

(4) Recalling past lives;

(5) Gaining an expanded consciousness which transcends the material level and includes great cycles of reincarnational manifestation;

(6) Identification of one's consciousness with a vast array of other forms of consciousness, including those of elemental spirits and dinosaurs;

(7) Experience of human/alien dual identity;

(8) Attainment of a multi-dimensional consciousness which seems to transcend the space-time matrix.

Let us deal with these items one at a time:

(1) The *falsehood* here is the identification of the willing surrender of one's ego with the forcible breaking of one's will. God is not a hypnotist or a terrorist. A deep and fertile relationship with the Source of All Life cannot be the product of brainwashing and mind-control. Therefore whatever forces employ such techniques are opposed to God. As C.S. Lewis writes in *The Screwtape Letters*, speaking through the mouth of his demon Screwtape:

> To us a human is primarily food; our aim is the absorption of its will into ours, the increase of our own area of selfhood at its expense. But the obedience which the Enemy demands of men is quite a different thing.... His service [is] perfect freedom.... We want cattle who can finally become food; He wants servants who can finally become sons.[1]

According to the Qur'an (2:256), 'there is no compulsion in religion.'

(2) The Jinn are, in a sense, intermediaries between the human state and higher conscious realms, simply because they inhabit a subtler plane of the Great Chain of Being—but to believe that they can be intermediaries *for us* is a *falsehood*: they are not on the 'human stem'. And if the Jinn we encounter happen to be what the Christians call 'fallen angels'—subtle-plane beings who have turned against the Source of Life through a perverted use of their free will—then they can only act as effective intermediaries between us and our own spiritual destruction. When Jesus said, 'none come to the Father but through me,' one of the things He meant was that no human being can unite with God by any other avenue than God's Humanity. As the Muslims say, human beings relate to God by virtue of our *fitrah*, our primordial, God-created human nature. Consequently, the image of God as an 'impersonal cosmic consciousness' is another *falsehood*. On the *first* level of the Great Chain of Being, God is Beyond Being, the unknowable Divine Essence, the 'Godhead' of the mystics; but we have no access to this Godhead except through the *second* level, through the personal God. And this God is not a separate Being, but is of one Essence with the Godhead. The Godhead is not impersonal,

1. New York: Macmillan, 1973, pp 37–38.

in other words, but *transpersonal;* if the Divine Personhood were not a potential within the Transpersonal Godhead, that Personhood could never appear. To believe otherwise is to identify self-transcendence and mystical Union with alienation and dehumanization. And this is an all-too-common counterfeit image of the spiritual Path in many people's minds, one which the aliens—as actual 'spirits of alienation'—are here to exploit.

(3) The ecstatic experience of a return 'Home'—a name for the aliens' point-of-origin which is taken directly from the motion picture *ET*, by the way—can only, given the horrific context, be a demonic *falsehood*. Because the aliens have access to the psychic plane, they can of course produce intense psychic experiences, as Mack repeatedly demonstrates; such experiences, as we well know, can even be initiated by chemicals. And given the hangover from materialism which still afflicts us, it is easier for them than ever before to palm off psychic experiences as Spiritual realiza-tions, since hardly anyone nowadays is taught even the need for a 'discernment of spirits', much less the necessary criteria, and since anything of a subtler quality than the dead material level of today's ambience will likely seem 'numinous'.

According to Dr Mack, most (but not all) UFO abductions appear to be 'out-of-body experiences'. Seraphim Rose has this to say of such experiences:

> It may be asked: What of the feelings of 'peace' and 'pleasantness' which seem to be almost universal in the 'out-of-body' state? What of the vision of 'light' which so many see?... These experiences are 'natural' to the soul when separated from the body.... In this sense the 'peace' and 'pleasantness' of the out-of-body experience may be considered real and not a deception. Deception enters in, however, the instant one begins to interpret these 'natural' feelings as something 'spiritual'—as though this peace were the true peace of reconciliation with God, and the 'pleasantness' were the true spiritual pleasure of heaven.[1]

1. *The Soul After Death* (Platina, CA: St Herman of Alaska Brotherhood, 1980), pp115–116.

(4; 5) Once again, transcendence of gross bodily consciousness is no proof of Spiritual development, or even of a valid Spiritual experience. And recall of past lives, as we have already seen, is a *falsehood* if taken literally. Furthermore, since it remains on the psychic plane alone, the plane of 'metempsychosis', it is in no way Spiritual.

(6) The identification of one's consciousness with a vast array of other types of consciousness is a mark of psychic dissolution, not spiritual development. The human mandate is first to realize one's total dependence upon God, and ultimately to see oneself with God's eyes, thereby becoming identified with the eternal Archetype of Humanity within the Divine Nature, the 'primordial Adam'. Through the eyes of this Divine Humanity, we can contemplate, and gain insight into, other forms of consciousness—organic, psychic and Spiritual; this is the meaning of the story in Genesis that 'Adam named the animals', and the similar story in the Qur'an that 'God told Adam the names of all created things': he saw into their essential natures, the Names of God which were, and are, their eternal archetypes. But to allow one's consciousness to flow horizontally into other non-human and sub-human forms via *a departure from the human form* is called 'insanity' on the psychic plane and 'damnation' on the Spiritual one. According to the Qur'an, after Allah created Adam, he commanded the angels to prostrate themselves to him. Every angel obeyed—except Iblis, the Muslim Satan. To open one's psyche to the endless variations of cosmic manifestation without remaining faithful to one's human form, as it exists in the mind of God, is to prostrate oneself to Iblis, and enter 'the darkness outside, where there will be weeping and gnashing of teeth.'

(7) The experience of human/alien dual identity is multiple-personality disorder on the psychic plane, and demonic possession on the Spiritual one. As the vampires of folklore turn their victims into vampires, so the alien kidnappers 'turn their victims into aliens' by 'stealing their souls'—by destroying their identification with their own humanity.

(8) The mark of true higher consciousness is Unity: 'Hear, O Israel, the Lord our God, the Lord is One.' The multidimensional kaleidoscope of the Jinn-world is destructive to Unity unless seen with the eyes of Unity: and only contemplative identification with

what is higher than us on the Great Chain of Being—not with dinosaurs, who are lower than us (not to mention being extinct!), or elemental spirits, who, though subtler than us, are not *central* like we are (being something like the sparks or reverberations of the Primordial Adam on the subtle material plane)—can give us those eyes.

The aliens are liars. As Mack himself admits, on p 415, 'I would not say that aliens never resort to deceptions to hide their purposes.' And one of their lies is that the reason they deliberately suppress abductees' memories of the abduction experience is to 'protect' their victims. (The real purpose, in my opinion, is to allow the seed of psychic control to mature undisturbed.) Mack, on the other hand, claims that he has seen no evidence that recall causes any harm. Shouldn't this in itself clue him in to the presence of deception? But of course, as he admits, deception presents no problems for him, and certainly hasn't led him to question the abductors' motives. Such naivete, in any other situation, would destroy the credibility as an objective researcher of the person exhibiting it. It does so here.

Mack's desire to be deceived seems to have completely destroyed his critical faculties, which is why he can make the following absurd and contradictory statement with, presumably, a straight face:

> Through [the aliens'] interaction with the abductees they bring them (and all of us potentially) closer to our spiritual cosmic roots, return us to the divine light or 'Home', a 'place' (really a state of being) where secrets, jealousy, greed, and destructiveness have no purpose. The aliens, on the other hand, long to experience the intense emotionality that comes with our full embodiment. They are fascinated with our sensuality, our warmth, our capacity for eroticism, and deep parental affection, and they seem to respond to openhearted love. They act at times like love-starved children. They delight in watching humans in all sorts of acts of love, which they may even stage as they stand around watching and chattering as the abductees perform them (pp 415–416).

At this point it seems almost unfair to take advantage of Dr Mack's vulnerability by pointing out the dizzying inconsistencies in the above passage—but duty calls: if the aliens come from a 'Home' where secrecy has no purpose, why do they so often keep their abductions secret by wiping all memory of them from the minds of their victims? If destructiveness has no purpose there, why are they so destructive, physically, socially and psychologically, to those unfortunate enough to encounter them? If they delight in our parental affection, why is alienation of affection between parents and children often one of the after-effects of abduction (p30)? And what does voyeuristically watching if not pornographically staging acts of human sexual intercourse have to do with love?

'The human/alien relationship itself evolves into a powerful bond' says Mack.

> Despite their resentment and terrorization, the abductees may feel deep love toward the alien beings, especially toward the leader figures, which they experience as reciprocated, despite the cold and business-like way the abductions themselves are conducted. The aliens may be perceived as true family, having protected the experiencers from human depredations, disease and loss (p416).

But Mack, in the very same book, has documented how the aliens themselves commonly produce disease and loss! Again we are shown, with nauseating clarity, how denial is only a virtue to the true believer.

The 'powerful bond' some abductees develop with their tormenters is, of course, no proof that the relationship is healthy, because—as we all know— *evil tempts*. C.S. Lewis, in *That Hideous Strength* (pp268–269), provides this chillingly accurate description of the demonic temptation of his hero by forces of the Antichrist:

> Suddenly, like a thing that leaped to him across infinite distances with the speed of light, desire (salt, black, ravenous, unanswerable desire) took him by the throat. The merest hint will convey to those who have felt it the quality of the emotion which now shook him, like a dog shaking a rat; for others, no description will perhaps avail. Many writers speak of it in terms of lust: a description admirably illuminating from within, totally misleading from without.... Everything else that Mark had ever

> felt—love, ambition, hunger, lust itself—appeared to have been mere milk and water, toys for children, not worth one throb of the nerves. The infinite attraction of this dark thing sucked all other passions into itself: the rest of the world appeared blenched, etiolated, insipid, a world of white marriages and white masses, dishes without salt, gambling for counters.... But it was like lust in another respect also. It is idle to point out to the perverted man the horror of his perversion: while the fierce fit is on, the horror is the very spice of his craving. It is ugliness itself that becomes, in the end, the goal of his lechery; beauty has long since grown too weak a stimulant. And so it was here. The creatures... breathed death on the human race and on all joy. Not despite but because of this the terrible gravitation sucked and tugged and fascinated him towards them.

Significantly, Mack finds that 'Virtually every abductee receives information about the destruction of the earth's ecosystem and feels compelled to do something about it' (p413). The aliens sometimes ask the abductees why they are so destructive; for some reason the abductees usually do not think to ask the same question of them. Abductees are very often shown horrendous images of future ecological devastation, and even of the actual splitting and disintegration of the globe, and emerge more 'environmentally sensitive' than they were before.

The 'human/alien hybridization program' is presented by the aliens as a response to the state of the environment. According to Mack,

> Both men and women come to feel despite their anger [at being abducted] that they are taking part—even that they have chosen to participate—in a process that is life-creating and life-giving. Furthermore, for most abductees the hybridization has occurred simultaneously with an enlightenment imparted by the alien beings that has brought home forcibly to them the failure of the human experiment in its present form. Abduction experiencers come to feel deeply that the death of human beings and countless other species will occur on a vast scale if we continue on our present course and that some sort of new life-form must evolve if

the human biological and spiritual essence is to be preserved. *They generally do not question why the maintenance of human life must take such an odd form* (pp 414–415; italics mine).

But of course a hybridization which appears to be happening on the subtle plane is not biological, nor is the essence of the alien/human hybrids really human, any more than that of the humanized ape produced in Italy in the 1980s, in which ape and human DNA were combined. In both cases, the result is a direct betrayal of the human essence, not its preservation. (Here we have good evidence, incidentally, that the demonic forces known as 'aliens' may in fact be providing the inspiration for the science of genetic engineering, particular when it is applied to human beings. It's as if the geneticists, virtually all of whom believe that man evolved from ape-like ancestors, are somehow being forced to prove, in actual practice, the doctrines of their traditionalist opponents, who assert—as does the Mayan book the *Popol Vuh*, among other ancient texts and traditions—that apes are really degenerate men.)

And the images of the Earth splitting in two provided by the aliens are curious. No amount of humanly-produced environmental devastation could have this effect. Apart from being a possible image of the 'cracks in the downward direction' in the 'great wall' spoken of by Guénon, one logical conclusion would be that such images are being used to terrorize us to the point where we will sacrifice our sexuality, and our humanity itself, to the alien terrorists who show them to us; the self-castration of members of the Heaven's Gate cult may have the same significance. They are apparently using our legitimate fear of environmental destruction and the end of the world to confront us with a temptation which can be summarized as follows:

Nature is more important than the human form—therefore abandon your humanity, betray the human archetype which is placed directly above you in the Divine Nature, and worship instead what is below you. Do not return sexuality to its archetype in God, via normal human love and reproduction; give your erotic, emotional and reproductive energies instead to the demonic and the infra-human. If you do this you can avoid God's judgement; you can avoid the confrontation with the Divine archetype of your Humanity, and not have to see how you have fallen away from it and betrayed it; you can avoid death, or at least species death; the human form can still live (the lie goes) *in sub-human form, as a demonic/human hybrid. If you want to avoid being sent to Hell, simply go to Hell on your own.*

They are imposing this temptation by means of the deepest and most intense of human emotions: life-creating sexual passion, and the fear of universal death. As any good brainwasher knows, terror is one of the two most effective tools for breaking the subject's will; *relief* is the other. And when terror is intense, sometimes sexual desire is the only refuge from it. Knowing this, the aliens produce the greatest fear of which they are capable, and then offer sexual desire as a way out. By this method they appropriate the sexuality of their victims, and gain a degree of power over them which is extremely hard to counter, since if an attempt to break free is proposed, the victim fears that the terror will return.

'The aliens stress the evolutionary aspect of the species-joining process, the repopulation of the Earth subsequent to a total environmental collapse' says Mack (p417). But then what becomes of the 'environmental sensitivity' the aliens reportedly produce in their victims? What good is environmental sensitivity in a dead world? And how can one love the earth, and wish to preserve it, if one's 'love of the earth' is the product of abduction, terror, and violation of one's human integrity? What experience could be better designed to make us *hate* the earth, and despair of doing anything to save it? What better way to make environmentalism repellent to religious believers than to associate it in their minds with demonic activity? And what better way to subvert environmentalism itself than to set up a false opposition between humanity and nature by claiming that the only way organic life—including human life—can survive is if we abandon our humanity? If the 'human experiment' has failed in its present form, if total environmental collapse is inevitable, then who's going to be motivated to preserve the natural world? And how can action to preserve the natural world be trusted to be environmentally healthy if carried on by someone with such a negative system of beliefs? Do we hire someone to reorganize our business who tells us up front that he's convinced we're going to fail? In view of this mass of deception designed to misrepresent their motives, I can only conclude that the real aim of the 'aliens' is to use our fear of the end of the world, and our guilt for destroying it, as an opportunity to lure us to our damnation.

So this is the triple demonic temptation of the latter days: (1) To worship the natural world in itself rather than worshipping God by means of it; (2) To divert our sexual powers in a sub-human direction; and (3), To directly betray the human form. And the three are intimately related, since to divert our powers of reproduction and the profound human emotions which are a natural aspect of them in a non-human direction is perhaps the most effective way of betraying our humanity; and to betray our humanity is the most effective way of destroying the earth, since our abdication of the God-given responsibility to act as His vicegerent in the material world is at the basis of our worship of sub-human ideologies, including materialism; and materialism is the worldview out of which have sprung the sub-human technologies which are destroying our planet. 'Where man is not, nature is barren,' said William Blake—to which the aliens reply, in effect, 'If dehumanization is destroying the earth, maybe *total* dehumanization can save it,' while simultaneously diverting our attention, for a moment at least, from the fact that they have already told us that it *can't* be saved: subliminal contradiction in its most terminal form. Fortunately, from all indications the alien 'visitors' are not to be believed. They are not reliable teachers—to say the very least. And sometimes the aliens themselves admit this. In an account by Jacques Vallee, humanoid aliens told an abductee that they contact people by chance, that they 'want to puzzle people,' and ordered him 'not to speak wisely about this night.'[1] If Dr Mack had been the abductee, I'm sure he would have been only too glad to comply with this directive.

1. *The Invisible College: What a Group of Scientists has Discovered about UFO Influences on the Human Race* (NY: Dutton, 1975), pp17, 21.

A COUNTERFEIT SECOND COMING

The myth of the UFO holds great power over the contemporary mind; it is a true sign of our times. This is due to the fact that, for all its sinister implications, there is an archetypal reality behind it. To take one example, even though UFOs appear in many different shapes—Jacques Vallee in *UFO Chronicles of the Soviet Union*[1] says that Russian UFOlogists are more willing than their Western counterparts to admit that the phenomenon is 'polyvalent'—the shining disk known as the 'flying saucer' has exercised more influence on the popular imagination than any other. Why is this?

Carl Jung, in *Flying Saucers: A Modern Myth of Things Seen in the Sky* (1959), saw in their circular shape a symbol of his 'Self Archetype', and thought that the phenomenon represented a collective longing for the Second Coming of Christ—a longing which, in my opinion, is being co-opted by the Jinn who serve Antichrist, and diverted, through collective fascination, toward a satanic counterfeit of the *parousia*.

Many UFOlogists, Erich van Däniken among them, have interpreted the vision of God's Throne in the first chapter of *Ezekiel* as a UFO manifestation, based on the brightness and swiftness of the 'four living creatures' (*hayoth*) who supported the Throne, and on the association of the creatures with 'wheels' and 'rings full of eyes' and 'a wheel within a wheel'. But Ezekiel's vision was not a sensual vision of meaningless and deliberately paradoxical aerial acrobatics produced by the Jinn, but an *intellectual* vision of God's creative power manifesting in, and as, the universe. If the Throne appeared to his physical eyes, it was only because the *meaning* of the Throne had already dawned upon his heart.

Leo Schaya, in *The Universal Meaning of the Kabbalah*, gives the symbolic meaning of Ezekiel's vision, which ought to be sufficient to allow anyone with the slightest degree of spiritual intuition see the vast difference in *level* between the UFO phenomenon and a true *theophany*:

1. Jacques Vallee in collaboration with Martine Castello, *UFO Chronicles of the Soviet Union: A Cosmic Samizdat* (NY: Ballantine, 1992).

> The 'throne', in its fullness, is the first and spiritual crystallization of all creatural possibilities before they are set in motion in the midst of the cosmos. When the 'throne' assumes its dynamic aspect and cosmic manifestation begins to move, it is called the divine 'chariot' (*merkabah*); then the four *hayoth*, or peripheral axes of creation, spring from the 'throne' become 'chariot', like 'lightning darting in all directions,' measuring all the dimensions and all the planes of manifested existence. Under the aspect of 'torches', 'brilliant lights' or spiritual 'flashes' of lightning, the *hayoth* are also called *kerubim* [cherubim], 'those who are close' to the living God, that is to say who emanate directly from God in action. While the hayothic axes are traveling in all the directions of the cosmos, out of them come 'wheels' (*ofanim*), or angelic powers, which play a part in actualizing the spherical forms and cyclical movements of the created; their spiral vibrations—as it were 'a wheel within another wheel'—are called 'whirlwinds' (*galgalim*).[1]

As the Antichrist counterfeits Christ, so the UFOs counterfeit God's Throne, which in Muslim as well as Hebrew metaphysics represents the apex of the created order, and in Christian terms appears as the 'Throne of the Lamb' at the center of the Heavenly Jerusalem.

The aliens are here to mimic Spiritual realities on the psycho-physical level, and so prepare the way for Antichrist. As St Symeon the New Theologian says in the *Philokalia* (p11),

> Men will not understand that the miracles of Antichrist have no good, rational purpose, no definite meaning, that they are foreign to truth, filled with lies, that they are a monstrous, malicious, meaningless play-acting, which increases in order to astonish, to reduce to perplexity and oblivion, to deceive, to seduce, to attract by the fascination of a pompous, empty, stupid effect.[2]

1. *The Universal Meaning of the Kabbalah* (Hillsdale, NY: Sophia Perennis, 2005), p74.
2. Quoted in *Orthodoxy and the Religion of the Future*, p145.

As our taste in art, architecture, social forms and human relationships is jaded in these latter days, so is our taste in miracles. According to Seraphim Rose,

> Serious scientists in [the former] Soviet Union . . . speculate that Jesus Christ may have been a 'cosmonaut', and that 'we today may be on the threshold of a 'second coming' of intelligent beings from outer space. (Sheila Ostrander and Lynn Schroeder, *Psychic Discoveries Behind the Iron Curtain*, Bantam Books, 1977. pp98–99). . . . Perhaps never since the beginning of the Christian era have demons appeared so openly and extensively as today. The 'visitors from outer space' theory is but one of the many pretexts they are using to gain acceptance for the idea that 'higher beings' are now to take charge of the destiny of mankind . . . the 'message' of the UFOs is: prepare for Antichrist; the 'savior' of the apostate world is coming to rule it. Perhaps he himself will come in the air, in order to complete his impersonation of Christ (Matt. 24:30; Acts 1:2); perhaps only the 'visitor from outer space' will land publicly in order to offer 'cosmic' worship of their master; perhaps the 'fire from heaven' (Rev. 13:13) will be only part of the great demonic spectacles of the last times. At any rate, the message for contemporary mankind is: expect deliverance, not from the Christian revelation and faith in an unseen God, but from vehicles in the sky.[1]

To avoid being drawn into the camp of the Antichrist, we must overcome, with God's help, the triple temptation presented above. We must *remember* that the forms of nature are not to be worshipped, but rather that we are called upon to worship the invisible and transcendent God by means of them, recognizing them as symbolic manifestations of eternal realities hidden within the Divine Nature. As St Paul says, 'For the invisible things of Him from the creation of the world are clearly seen, being understood by the things that are made, even His eternal power and Godhead' (Rom. 1:20).

1. *Orthodoxy and the Religion of the Future*, pp102, 140–42.

We must *remember* the sacredness and symbolic depth of our sexual powers and natures. In the words of James Cutsinger:

> [What C.S. Lewis calls] this 'real polarity' [of gender] is to be found, not only as Lewis suggests in creatures, however superhuman, but all the way up to the Divine Reality itself... which is the ultimate Source of everything else, and which for that reason is the source and paradigm of all distinctions. In its absoluteness and transcendence, the Divine is the archetype for everything masculine, while its infinity and capacity for immanence are displayed at every level of the feminine ... the polar qualities revealed to us as sex are actually and objectively on every plane of the ontological hierarchy.... As Seyyed Hossein Nasr has written, 'The difference between the two sexes cannot be only biological and physical, because in the traditional perspective the corporeal level of existence has its principle in the subtle state, the subtle in the spiritual, and the spiritual in the Divine Being itself.[1]

Gender is in fact so integral to our humanity that the way in which we live it out, or sublimate it, or dedicate it, is one of the things which determines whether or not we remain united with our human archetype. To let our sexuality fall into the power of non-human forces is to depart from the human form. To dedicate it to a fully human love, or directly to God as in the monastic vocation, is to worship God by means of the human form.

Lastly, we must *remember* what the human form really is. Allah, in the *ahadith qudsi* (the traditions in which God Himself speaks), declares that 'Heaven and earth cannot contain Me, but the heart of my believing slave can contain Me.' And in the words of St Gregory of Nyssa:

> Know to what extent the Creator has honoured you above all the rest of creation. The sky is not an image of God, nor is the

1. 'Femininity, Hierarchy and God' in *Religion of the Heart*, ed., Seyyed Hossein Nasr and William Stoddart, p115 (Washington DC: Foundation for Traditional Studies, 1991).

> moon, nor the sun, nor the beauty of the stars, nor anything of what can be seen in creation. You alone have been made the image of the Reality that transcends all understanding, the likeness of imperishable beauty, the imprint of true divinity, the recipient of beatitude, the seal of true light. When you turn to him you become that which he is himself.... There is nothing so great among beings that it can be compared with your greatness. God is able to measure the whole heaven with his span. *The earth and the sea are enclosed in the hollow of his hand. And although he is so great and holds all creation in the palm of his hand, you are able to hold him,* he dwells in you and moves within you without constraint....'[1]

According to esoteric teachings from many traditions, clearly reflected in the above passages, humanity is the 'stem' connecting the earth to God. God sustains the earth and all that is in it only through man—a doctrine which is proved negatively by the fact that man alone has the power to destroy the earth: when we no longer take God as our center, and so depart from our own humanity, the earth begins to die. It is this truth, above all, that the aliens are doing all in their power to prevent us from remembering.

Nothing happens that is not God's will. Nonetheless, according to Sufi metaphysician Ibn al-'Arabi, even though all that happens is willed by God—because if it were possible for something contrary to His will to occur, He would not be God—not everything is part of God's *wish.* This is why He sends us sacred laws, which let us know what to do and what to avoid if we want to come nearer to Him. Evil is not good in itself; it is contrary to God's wish. But he wills it—or, in Christian terms, allows it—as part of a greater good. We don't curse the worms that devour a dead body; and from a certain perspective the 'aliens' are nothing but worms, whose job is to devour whatever is already dead in the human collective psyche. But that doesn't mean that it is a good idea to spend your time

1. *Second Homily on the Song of Songs* (PG 44, 765); italics mine. Quoted in *The Roots of Christian Mysticism*, by Olivier Clément (New York: New City Press, 1995), p79.

socializing with dead bodies; if you do, you will become ill. The experience of disease is a natural evil, and abduction, torture and rape are moral ones—which, to the victim, are nonetheless morally indistinguishable from natural disasters. Yet such evils, if we encounter them with a deep enough faith in our Creator, can sharpen our spiritual vigilance, and ultimately awaken us to a deeper Mercy. Just as lies testify to the Truth—not because they are true, but because the ability to recognize their falsehood is a sign of Truth's presence—so misfortune and catastrophe testify to Mercy. Even the worst sufferings can be known, God willing, as part of a Mercy which is so great that even this—even war, even cancer, even alien abduction—is swallowed up in it. As it says in the *ahadith qudsi*, 'My Mercy precedeth my Wrath'; and in the Qur'an: 'There is no refuge from God but in Him.'

MEMOIR AND CONCLUSION

SINCE I HAVE CHOSEN to write about the UFO phenomenon, perhaps the reader is wondering whether I have any direct experience of the phenomenon myself. The answer is: in a small way, yes.

In the early 1970s, when my spiritual practice was entirely 'experimental' and self-directed, I decided to do a spiritual retreat on Mt Shasta in northern California, a mountain sacred to the original Native American inhabitants, and also considered to be a 'power spot' by every occultist, Neo-pagan, and New Age group under the sun. I traveled there with two friends, drove up the mountain as far as the road went, and then hiked in, arriving at Horse Camp, set in a sea of fragrant 'Shasta tea' (pennyroyal), and high enough on the mountain to give an unobstructed and stunning view. For three days I ate nothing but brown rice, and also observed a vow of silence.

On one of the nights I spent on the mountain, I had a significant dream—perhaps my first 'lucid dream' (a dream in which the dreamer 'wakes up' to the fact that he is dreaming) since early childhood. In the dream I was gleefully aware that, since I was 'only' dreaming, I could now do anything I wanted—though the ironic look on the face of the woman I met seemed to say, 'yes, but not without consequences.' (Only after a certain amount of hard experience in later years did I begin to understand the meaning of that look.)

One evening, shortly after the sun disappeared behind a distant range of mountains, I sat meditating, facing west. In those days I used to meditate with my eyes open, and this evening, as I slipped into a light trance, I saw two points of light crossing the western sky, from right to left. The light they gave off was somehow more precise, more defined, more 'real' than ordinary light. (Spectrographic analysis of the light emanating from certain UFOs has since revealed it to be richer in various blended wavelengths of visible radiation than light from any known 'natural' source.) As soon as I noticed them, I became alert, attentive; I rose out of trance, back to full waking consciousness – and the lights disappeared. Then I relaxed, centered my energy, sank back into a meditative state again—and there they were. I realized through this experience that UFOs habitually exist on a subtler plane of existence than the material—a plane which, however, is very close to the material and capable of impinging on it. The 'craft' in question were not visible to my full waking consciousness, but neither were they mental images. They existed in a layer of reality that somehow came between psychic and the material—what some have called the 'etheric plane'. (In later years I used the 'etheric sight' I had began to develop during my retreat on Mt. Shasta to investigate—in other words, to meddle with—the world of the Nature Spirits.)

It is interesting that my one and only sighting of UFOs coincided with the first lucid dream of my adult life. (I continued to experience lucid dreaming and/or 'astral projection' for years, and finally became involved in attempts to deliberately produce it, basing them partly on *Lucid Dreaming* by Dr Stephen LeBerge of Stanford University, as well as the books of Carlos Castaneda and Jane Roberts. It was only after my initiation into a traditional Sufi order than my lucid dream experiences finally stopped.) Lucid dreaming involves a partial erasure of the border between waking consciousness and dream consciousness, between material and psychic reality; the self-reflexive awareness of the waking state—or something similar to it—now has as its object not the world reported by the five senses but the subtle psychic environment.

All this was very interesting to me at the time. It seemed like a harmless excursion into the wonders of the etheric and psychic worlds, magical worlds where the Imagination ruled, and where that Imagination, in all its subjectivity, could finally be 'objectively' validated. And if these worlds, at least to begin with, were 'magical' to me more in the Walt Disney than in the Aliester Crowley sense of the word, I was to discover in later years that the heavy, humorless and sinister aspects of these subtle planes could not ultimately be avoided.

Jumping ahead to November of the year 2003, I was interviewed on the syndicated radio program *A Closer Look*, hosted by Michael Corbin, on the subject of my book *The System of Antichrist: Truth and Falsehood in Postmodernism and the New Age*, from which much of the present book is excerpted. I don't know what he and our listeners may have learned from me, but I learned from him a very interesting thing: that, according to his own research, most of the people who claim to have been abducted by UFO aliens admit to having dabbled in the occult. Then, around a month later, I discovered on the website, in the archives of Corbin's programs, a report of a recent UFO sighting in Morehead, Kentucky. An investigator from MUFON (the Mutual UFO Network) was interviewed. She reported that a brilliant light had descended from the sky, shortly after which a women's bloodcurdling screams were heard by several people in the area—though no missing person reports were filed and no-one had as yet turned up whom the screams could be connected to. Cell phone trouble was also reported during the incident, and three electric clocks stopped permanently. Now Morehead is where my wife's uncle lives with his wife and daughter; so she rang them up to ask if they had heard of the incident, and discovered that they lived only a stone's throw from the road where some of those who saw the UFO lived. Her aunt said that she had neither witnessed nor heard of the sighting—but that ever since the date of the report, their own cell phones had been acting up.

So what I once thought of as harmless psychic entertainment—or, alternatively, as my first few serious steps on the spiritual Path—has now been revealed as a kind of uncanny terror, a terror striking all too close to home. As I have already pointed out, René Guénon, in *The Reign of Quantity and the Signs of the Times*, spoke of cracks in the Great Wall separating the material plane from the subtle plane as a sign of the approaching end of this cycle of manifestation, cracks which initially appear in the downward direction, producing a destructive influx of 'infra-psychic' forces. And on reviewing the history of my own 'explorations' of psychic worlds in the name of spiritual development, I am led to speculate whether the very paradigm I was operating on might be in some way related to this infra-psychic invasion.

The spiritual Path exists in an environment of Grace, specifically that initiatory Grace which the Sufis call *baraka*. Before we desire God, God must have desired us; both the initial call and the ultimate acceptance emanate from the pole of the Divine. Between this call and this acceptance, much work needs to be done by the spiritual traveler; yet the work is essentially the work of obedience, of active response to God's Grace. All that is needed to walk the path is given by God; our work is simply to assimilate what has been freely given.

The exact reverse of this is the paradigm of magic: Power is there, and it is up to us to break our way in to those worlds where power resides, to access it and use it. We can employ it (so the story goes) either to "take heaven by storm," or to obtain security, pleasure and power in this world; what we use it for is entirely up to us. (In reality, of course, we cannot take heaven by storm, nor can we employ magic to fulfill our worldly desires without dire and most likely permanent consequences; see the Parable of the Wedding Feast in Matthew 22:1–14.) In any case, we must access power entirely on our own initiative. In the process we may tap 'allies', 'entities', 'familiar spirits', who may guide us on our way, but their power to guide has nothing to do with any responsibility on our part to obey what is higher than us on the Great Chain of Being, to sacrifice our self-will in service to the Divine Will. These entities are more like repositories of useful information which we must struggle to contact and dominate, ultimately forcing them to divulge their secrets, by hook or by crook. And the program of 'penetrating' the etheric and psychic planes, through various intense psycho-physical practices, as well as the use of psychedelic drugs, in order to explore them and make use of the energies they are composed of—and this certainly includes attempts to "control" the dream-state—is not spiritual practice: it is magic.

I now believe that it is largely the attempt by so many people today to penetrate the higher planes of existence from below, on the basis of a magical self-will, rather of responding obediently to a Grace descending from above, that widens those cracks in the Great Wall now opening in the downward direction. In other words, it is the magical will to break in to the higher worlds which allows infra-psychic, demonic forces to break in to this world from below.

The cold, sizzling, electrical energy of the UFO phenomenon (I'm speaking impressionistically here) seems specifically designed to devastate the nourishing emotional matrix of the human world—in other words, to destroy love. The Grace that descends from the higher worlds, and invites us to follow it—by God's own leave, and in His own time—is inseparable from love, precisely because God Himself is Love. The ripping away of our natural psychic protections, on the other hand, the breaching of our psycho-physical energy fields so our vital and emotional energy can bleed away into uncanny, alien worlds is the very opposite of love, though it is of the very essence of magic. (NOTE: let anyone who wants a graphic portrayal of how magic destroys love, rent and view the Russian motion picture *Shadows of our Forgotten Ancestors.*) Like sexual promiscuity, the practice of dabbling in psychic and magical techniques may rupture the energetic and emotional self-containment which allows us to relate to others without losing our spiritual center, our inviolable human integrity; such 'discretion' is a necessary part of self-respect, without which no love worthy of the name is possible. And if discretion is necessary for love to exist between human beings, it is all the more necessary in the relationship between the soul and God. The 'co-dependency' exhibited by UFO abductees in relation to their abductors is nothing more than an especially intense case of the general lack of spiritual center exhibited by postmodern humanity. If we do not know God, we cannot be ourselves; if we are not ourselves, then we are dead meat for any entity from the infra-psychic realm who wants a slice of us. Buffy the Vampire Slayer would do better to practice the virtue of discretion, develop some basic self-respect, and learn to mind her own business. But this is effectively is impossible without a fundamental faith in God, expressed through the ability to focus one's attention on Absolute Truth and Love. That's the only way the spooks and entities, the vampires and UFO aliens who beset us in today's world can be definitively overcome: by starving them to death. Those whose subtle attention has not yet awakened may still be relatively immune to the UFO influence—though as René Guénon says in *The Reign of Quantity*, the illusion of 'ordinary life' which used to protect us from such incursions is fast breaking down. As for the rest of us, if our subtle attention is not reserved for God alone, it will be abducted, to one degree or another, by the forces of the infra-psychic. In other words, the perennial choice between obeying God and yielding to temptation is today being presented to us in a new guise: on the one hand, an attention to God which is both conscious and constant; on the other, an obsession with the demonic, usually unconscious, but in some cases conscious and deliberate. Our basic weapon against the alien invasion, then, is the spiritual practice known as *recollection*: the practice of gathering together the scattered energy of our subtle attention, withdrawing it from the many psychic worlds into which it has wandered, and placing it upon God alone.

Printed in Great Britain
by Amazon